# ryan giggs
## genius at work

by ryan giggs, alex leith & jim drewett

ANDRE
DEUTSCH

# ryan giggs
## genius at work

### by ryan giggs, alex leith & jim drewett

Thanks to Harry Swales
Ben and Matt Ayres

Photos:
Action Images
John Rogers/FSP
John Peters
Sportshot
Empics
Sporting Pictures

Written by Alex Leith and Jim Drewett, Deadline
Design by Andy Smith
Text research by Clive Batty
Picture research by Justyn Barnes
Statistical research by Louise Pepper
Sub-edited by Nicky Hodge

First published in 1996 by Manchester United Books
An imprint of André Deutsch Ltd, 106 Great Russell Street, London WC1B 3LJ
in association with
Manchester United Football Club plc, Old Trafford, Manchester M16 0RA
Copyright @ 1996 Manchester United Football Club

CIP data available from the British Library
ISBN 0233990461

Printed in Italy

A Zone Production

# genius at work

# contents

**prologue**

OK. So you look at me, 23 years of age, playing for the best club in the world, all the domestic trophies there are under my belt and you think "lucky so-and-so", right? You're not the only one: so do I.

I feel incredibly proud to be where I am today, involved in the set-up at Manchester United. Incredibly proud and incredibly lucky. Lucky that I was spotted when I was, lucky to have been trained and educated in the way I have been, lucky to have the best mum in the world, lucky to have been born with quick legs and a deft left foot.

This book doesn't tell you that I first encountered a football in my back garden and started kicking it round with my dad when I lived in Cardiff, before I moved to Manchester aged seven in 1981. But it does tell you more or less everything else about my career, from my first break – when I got into the Grosvenor Road Primary school team – to my greatest success, winning the double Double with Manchester United in May 1996.

Along the way there have been a lot of people who have helped me (and hindered me) in getting where I am today. There have been a lot of incidents, both bad and good, and a lot of team-mates have come and gone at Old Trafford. But above all, there have been a lot of football matches.

This book is about those football matches and the periods between them in which various people have helped to shape my career – international and domestic – into what it has become. It is a book about football. It is not about the private side of Ryan Giggs. My private life is something I want to keep to myself. It's not a big deal: I just like going to the local pub with the mates I've known since I was 11 or so, as I explain later. If you want to know about my boozy nights in night-clubs all over the world with glamourous blondes on my arm, read the tabloids. What they write may not be the truth, but I tell you, it's a hell of a lot more interesting than what I do get up to off the football pitch.

If you're interested in hearing my thoughts about my career so far, about playing for Wales (and not England), about the pressures of being a professional sportsman, about what it's like to be Ryan Giggs the footballer, read on. It's been a great life so far, so it should be a pretty good book.

the best yet?

chapter one

Back in 1991/92, when Ryan Giggs was first making a name for himself as a precocious 17-year-old winger on the fringe of the Manchester United team, something terrible happened. He was compared with George Best.

Giggs did have a lot in common with the Irishman. Both liked to wear the number 11 shirt and both were wingers whose uncanny skills enabled them to leave defenders behind, making the pitch look as if it were made of greased banana skins. They also both had a knack for scoring goals.

Giggs wasn't the first player to be compared to the Irishman – not by a long chalk. Any talented youngster starting out at United had people drooling over the possibility of another player with Best's finesse emerging in the English Football League. It had happened to Willie Morgan, Sammy McIlroy, Gordon Hill, Norman Whiteside and, more recently, Lee Sharpe. It had even happened to Peter Marinello at Arsenal. Sometimes, it seemed, the comparisons had been enough to mar careers for ever; other players had been strong enough to come out intact with reputations of their own.

One thing that marked Best out from his peers – and which eventually led to his downfall – was that he wasn't just incredibly talented. He was very good-looking too. Giggs was the first newcomer since Best capable of making both grown men and grown women go weak at the knees. The stage looked set for another footballing career spoilt because of fast cars and fast women. Luckily, however, Giggs concentrated his energies on ruining opposing defenders' reputations, rather than his own.

From the start of his career at United, Giggs distinguished himself on the playing field, with some stunning performances that turned him from unknown apprentice to household name in a matter of months. One man who has constantly praised him throughout his career – a man who doesn't like wasting his words – is the United manager. "His ability is heaven sent," says Ferguson, before adding, without mentioning Best's name, that "a footballer of his calibre pops up maybe once in a couple of generations."

"He's a defender's worst nightmare," continues Ferguson. "It's chilling the way Ryan seems to float over the surface rather than run like the rest of us. So light on his feet and blessed with wonderful, wonderful balance. I can't stress that quality too much. He is so quick and checks with that instant stop that makes you think he was born with an ABS braking system in his feet. Whatever the secret, markers just can't live with him. They are falling all over the place and he is still on his feet ready for the next one."

George Best himself is a big Giggs fan, and he too singled out the Welsh teenager's sense of equilibrium as a major asset. "The one thing great athletes have is perfect balance. Ryan has it, and that's why he doesn't get hurt in tackles." "If there is one thing that separates him from other promising youngsters and gives him a real chance of being an all-time great it is his balance – it is glorious," agrees Bryan Robson, for so long Giggs' skipper and one of his boyhood idols.

His pace, too, is something that sets him apart from other players. It was the first thing United forward Brian McClair noticed about Giggs when he played with him in a practice match when the apprentice was only 15. "I remember him getting the ball and running 60 yards with it before delivering a cross," says the Scottish international. "I couldn't believe his speed. I wasn't there to meet the cross because I hadn't been able to keep up with him – and he was running with the ball at his feet, I wasn't."

Former Everton defender Kevin Ratcliffe played against Giggs on his United debut and with him on his debut for Wales a few months later. Ratcliffe remembers the young winger's pace particularly well: "Fullbacks like to go very close to young wingers, to get an early tackle in and not give them an inch of space. But Ryan would actually go and mark the defenders, get very tight to them, so that he'd be right alongside if the ball was played over the top for him to run on to. That pace really worries defenders, it scares them. When you're facing him, up against that pace, you tend to think 'oh, hell!'"

Tim Flowers, the Blackburn and England goalkeeper, has been on the receiving end of plenty of Giggs magic. He is a little more poetic in his description of the winger: "He picks the ball up and runs the defence absolutely ragged. He comes down the pitch like a snake, side-winding all the way. It's frightening to think what he can achieve."

Pace isn't everything, of course. Linford Christie could outrun any Premiership defender, but he'd be hard-pressed to get into the Stockport second team. Giggs has the ability to do something special with the ball at the end of his runs, and he always seems to have plenty of options up his sleeve. "He's practically impossible to predict," adds Flowers. "You don't know if he'll come inside or shoot or dip outside and cross the ball. Speaking as a fan, I think he's pure magic. He's going to terrorise goalkeepers before he's through." McClair has often marvelled at Giggs' inventiveness with the ball. "There have been so many times when Giggs has surprised me it's hard to single out one occasion," he says. "Ryan produces all sorts of wonderful things that people wouldn't try on the training ground, let alone on the pitch."

Denis Irwin, United's regular left back, partners Giggs on the left flank. "When he's on form, there's nobody better than him in the game," he says. "He's obviously the sort of player we want to get the ball to because of what he can do to other teams, and what he's capable of creating. That's why the ball goes down the left quite a bit and it just so happens that if I play there we usually link up quite well."

One thing's for sure: only brilliant right backs relish the idea of playing against Giggs. England international Warren Barton, having played against Giggs both for Newcastle and Wimbledon, knows a thing or two about the Welshman's game. "He really is something special," he says. "Pace, control, superb balance, he's got the lot. I've faced him quite a few times now, and it's always been a really tough battle. He's a nice guy too. It's always a pleasure to play against him."

Wingers revel in taking the mickey out of fullbacks, which means they come in for a lot of stick from their opponents. Pace and ability aren't enough in the Premiership if you can't handle the pressure. Many a winger has faded out of the game because they were too lightweight. Not Giggs, as Alex Ferguson acknowledges. "Physically he might not look much, but he can certainly take care of himself on the park. When he looks your way on the pitch, he fixes you with those cold, unblinking eyes. They bore through you like lasers. There ain't nobody who'll make him twitch and tremble while he's wearing football boots. There is a soldier's courage in him and he is also as strong as a bull. Mentally and physically he is armour-plated – a very tough cookie indeed."

Soccer folklore is littered with memories of hugely talented players who have fallen by the wayside because they didn't have the right attitude. Giggs, especially after the comparisons with George Best, had all the credentials to join the list of the fallen, He's young, gifted and blessed with the sort of skills that can put millions in your bank account. Nevertheless, despite the fact that the press are dying to rake up any muck they can find on him, they haven't yet been able to find any that sticks. The guy's no angel – he enjoys the odd drink, he likes going out and having fun. He wouldn't be normal if he didn't. As Harold Wood, the United steward who discovered Giggs, points out: "You see things in the paper. But that's only the sort of thing lads of 19, 20, 21 do, isn't it? Fundamentally he's a sensible lad."

"Considering all the attention he gets he's a very normal young lad," says Brian McClair. "He likes to go out, he's still got a lot of friends from when he was at school. He's close to his family, too. There's nothing big-headed about him at all."

"Ryan hasn't been changed by fame and stardom," agrees his best friend Stuart Grimshaw, who has known him since he first played organised football at the age of 11. "It's remarkable really, because I think it would change a lot of people. He's very cool about it. He's still one of the lads when we see him. We just do normal things – play golf, watch telly or videos, play pool or just mess about. We have got a regular pub we can go to where Ryan is treated normally and nobody bothers him."

Ask anybody who knows Giggs about his attitude, and they'll all come out with a pretty similar answer. Former United star Sammy McIlroy says: "Ryan Giggs has had all this George Best stuff, like I had in the early days of my career, but to me he seems a very level-headed lad who can probably handle all the hype about him. I think he's a fantastic player – a world class player – but he's probably the first one to say that there was only one George Best, just like there's only one Ryan Giggs." Another United player of the same era, former skipper Martin Buchan, agrees: "His ability is amazing and he's got the perfect temperament for a player. I'm a really big fan of his."

The good temperament Giggs displays on the pitch is also displayed on the training field. Giggs

has a thirst to learn more about the game, something which will almost inevitably make him a better player. "He's a very special talent," says former teammate Mark Hughes. "He knows he has a lot to learn, but he's always willing to listen to the older players. Some of the younger ones don't, they just nod their heads and forget what you've just said." McClair agrees. "Giggs' attitude is spot-on," he says, "especially in training. He has a huge appetite for the game, and you can see he's enjoying himself. He works hard, too, and is willing to learn. He can only improve."

Part of Giggs' level-headedness must go down to Ferguson, who shielded him from the press when he started making his name at United. "Keeping Ryan away from the media was a good decision and I know that he appreciated it," says the manager. "He's been allowed to grow up within the game, and now that he knows what it's all about, he's becoming more visible and more confident."

With the amount of praise that's flying around Ryan Giggs, it must be pretty difficult to keep his head on his shoulders. Here's former United manager Ron Atkinson: "I would break the bank to buy Ryan Giggs tomorrow if I could. He makes you believe there is a football God after all." Here's another former United manager, Tommy Docherty: "He will never lose his world-class ability. People forget he's years away from his prime, which is frightening for defenders." Here's current manager Ferguson: "In football terms he's the hottest property in the game." And former United superstar Denis Law: "He's the jewel in the crown. I think the sky's the limit for Giggs. He's become a very, very talented player." And former Wales manager Terry Yorath: "There is no doubt he is an excellent player. I'm just glad he was born in Wales."

There's another connection with George Best. Best, born and bred in Belfast, never made it to a major international tournament because he played for Northern Ireland. Giggs has already missed out on two because Wales, for whom Terry Yorath made him the youngest player aged 17 years 332 days, failed to qualify for USA '94 and Euro '96. Like Best, we may never know what Giggs would be like at the highest level.

Giggs is obviously quite flattered by all the comparisons but, at the same time, quite sick of everybody trying to fit him into Best's number 11 shirt. He is happy be compared to his United forbear because, as he says, Bestie was one of the most talented footballers to come out of Britain. Denis Law goes a little bit further, trying to put an end to all the comparisons. "There's no way Ryan Giggs is another George Best," he says. "He's another Ryan Giggs." But it's down to Best himself to put the picture straight. "One day they might even say I was another Ryan Giggs," says the Irishman with a wink.

the boy's a bit special

# chapter two

One winter afternoon in 1986, a milkman called Dennis Schofield was driving his milk float back to the depot in Swinton, North Manchester. "I was passing Grosvenor Primary School and I saw a game going on," he remembers. "So I parked the float and went over to have a look at the match." Schofield was a scout for Manchester City. He ran a youth team, Deans, and was always interested in spotting new talent. That Friday afternoon, he was to stumble on something rather special. "There was a lad playing on the left wing who was far beyond the others," he remembers. "He was taking the ball up the wing, beating the fullback, showing a lot of confidence in himself – and he was quick." He was, of course, Ryan Wilson (later to change his name to Ryan Giggs). Even at nine years old he was noticeably better than his teammates.

"There were quite a few parents watching the game so I asked around to find out if either of the lad's parents were there," continues Schofield. "Somebody pointed out his mum and I went over to speak to her. I asked her if her son would like to play for my youth club team, Deans. She told me that they hadn't been in Swinton long and was more than happy for her sons, Ryan and his younger brother Rhodri, to come along. So Ryan started playing for Deans, and I used to go round his house to give the boys a lift down to the club."

In 1981, Ryan Wilson had moved to Swinton, a suburb to the North of Manchester, from Cardiff at the age of seven with his parents and younger brother. He was born in the Welsh capital on 29

November 1973. The family moved because Ryan's father, Danny Wilson, was a keen rugby player. Having made a handful of appearances as fly-half for Cardiff in 1975, he had been offered professional terms with Swinton Rugby League Club. Cardiff's club statistician Peter Nyam remembers Wilson senior well: "He was pretty nifty on his feet – quite an elusive character. He didn't really like the rough stuff, though, and wasn't quite top grade material." Wilson made a better impression at Swinton, and played for the club for several years. Ryan Wilson grew to like his new surroundings, but has never forgotten his birthplace.

**I love Cardiff. I lived in the city till I was seven, and didn't really want to move to Manchester. I used to go down to Cardiff every summer holiday though, and sometimes for the weekend, so I still kept in touch with the place. I was proud to be Welsh. When I moved to Manchester I had a Welsh accent. Other kids used to take the mickey, so I made sure I lost it. Very very quickly.**

**My first taste of serious football was at Grosvenor Road Primary School in Swinton. The school didn't teach football until the last year. I got into the team a year early so I played for two years, instead of one. I was a winger then, too. My strength was my pace. I just used to wait on the wing till the ball came to me, and run. I remember one match in particular. We were playing in a cup competition and we got to the final, which was a big deal at the time. We played in front of maybe 30 or 35 people, but it seemed like a huge crowd. We won. It was my first taste of glory.**

It was during a Grosvenor Road Primary game that he was spotted by Dennis Schofield, and started playing for Deans. His teammate, Stuart Grimshaw, recalls that Giggs was rather better than the others. "He was outstanding, a different class to the rest of us and exceptionally quick," he says. "We knew that if we got the ball to Ryan, we'd have a chance to score." Schofield knew he had a prodigious talent on his hands, and tried to improve Giggs' versatility from day one. "At Deans, I played him in virtually every position," says Schofield. "He wasn't using his right foot very much at first, so I put him on the right wing to encourage him to use his weaker foot and to get him cutting inside to shoot on his left. He was happy to play anywhere for us and even played a few games in goal. He was a good keeper, very agile and with good handling skills – later on he played basketball and rugby. The only position I wasn't too happy about him playing was as a wide midfielder. I wanted him further forward, attacking and beating full backs."

The next step on the footballing ladder was a trial at Salford Juniors.

I can remember going to the trial very well, even now. I didn't know anyone there. There were about 40 boys and they took us into the changing room. The names they didn't read out would make it into the next trial. It was really tense, listening to the names being read out and not wanting to hear yours. My name wasn't read out. There were about 28 boys left and we were put into an A and a B team. The A team were on first and they won 4–2. Then it was the B team. We won 8–1 and I scored six. They didn't pick me for the B team again.

It was the most serious football I had yet played. We used to travel all over the place, playing teams from Oldham and Liverpool and the like. These were the most organised games you could play at that age. We used to train once a week as well and play on Saturday morning. I was always playing with boys a year older than me. When I was 14, I was playing for the Under 16s and we got to the national final against St Helen's. We played at Old Trafford, which was magic. We lost, but it gave me my first taste of the big time. I knew I wanted to go back to play at that ground.

Of course, I had already been to Old Trafford many times – but as a fan, not a player. When I moved to Manchester I had to choose between Manchester United and Manchester City. I chose Man United because most of my friends were United fans. So I first went to Old Trafford when I was eight or nine. We were playing Stoke City. The only player I can remember was Micky Thomas, because he was Welsh.

From about 12 or 13 onwards I used to go every week. We'd travel on the bus and go and watch from the Stretford End. We used to sing and everything. There was a big gap

between the Stretford End and the other stand and we used to stand up there because you got a good view of the game. Sometimes we'd go down the bottom, where there was a better atmosphere but you couldn't see so much. My heroes were Mark Hughes and Bryan Robson. I had posters of them on my wall, along with Michel Platini. I loved Hughes for his spectacular goals and, of course, for the fact that he was Welsh. Robson was just the complete player.

But at that stage, it looked as though I was more likely to end up playing at Maine Road than Old Trafford. Dennis Schofield was a Manchester City scout. When I was 11, after a season of being in his team at Deans, he recommended me to a City School of Excellence. I used to go a couple of times a week to train with other players from Manchester. Most of the kids at the club were City fans, but I was there for about three years and I was always a Man United fan. I'd always turn up to training in a red T-shirt, even though it was banned.

Schofield, a devoted Manchester City fan, reckons young Ryan spent a little longer than he remembers with City. "More or less immediately after he joined Deans I took him along to Maine Road to train once or twice a week at City's School of Excellence," Schofield remembers. "He really enjoyed going there and was very impressed by the facilities. It was the first time he had seen inside a professional club. Sometimes I'd go along to the sessions to see how he was getting on. He was at City from the age of nine to 14. But it was obvious Manchester United knew about him too and were tracking him. Three or four times I saw people from Old Trafford watching him play. City, though, were anxious to keep him. Everybody thought he had great potential, and the feeling was that we had to keep hold of this lad."

Football wasn't the only sport I was playing at the time. I also played rugby – as a stand-off, like my Dad. It really toughened me up. I was playing for Salford, and we weren't the best of teams. We were being beaten 60–0 by the likes of St Helens. The lads I was playing were twice as big as me, but I never really got flattened. I managed to run my way out of trouble.

I had pretty busy weekends in those days. I used to play football for Salford Juniors in the morning, rugby with Salford in the afternoon, then rugby with a local side on Sunday morning followed by Sunday League football in the afternoon. I wasn't too knackered at the end of it, though. It strengthened me up, really – especially as I was always playing kids a year above me.

By this time he had moved schools – to Moorside High School in Swinton, largely considered to be the best of the three secondary schools in the area. His form tutor at Moorside was Dave Winnings, who remembers him fondly: "I used to work in a neighbouring school, and when I told one of my colleagues that I was moving to Moorside, he told me about Ryan, who he'd coached at Salford Juniors. He raved about the lad and said he was an absolute genius on the field. I took it with a pinch of salt, but when I arrived at the school and saw him play football, I found it was true. He was head and shoulders above the other kids. He was a remarkable footballer.

"Ryan was a very quiet lad," continues Winnings, "very polite, too. He had a huge amount of respect from his colleagues because of his athletic prowess. When he was in what we then called the fourth and fifth year, he excelled at all sports at a time when a lot of other lads were starting to tire of them and go into couch-potato mode. I remember very well that we had an annual sports day, and that the kids were only allowed to go in for two events. Ryan was so good we bent the rules for him. He wanted to compete in events that nobody else wanted to do, like the 440 metres, which was considered a bit heavy going. He won everything of course. He was an excellent sprinter and a fine athlete."

Winnings was also Giggs' art teacher. "Art wasn't his forte, to tell you the truth," he reports. "I remember when he had to draw still-life compositions he was always more interested in copying his partner's drawing than trying to depict the subject. He was a very hard-working lad, though, and he passed his art exam in the end."

It was remarkable that Giggs had any time for schoolwork with the amount of sport he was playing. But it paid off in the end, especially when he came to realise his dream of playing for Manchester United.

**The mother of one of the lads in my Sunday League team used to know one of the top stewards at Manchester United. His name was Harold Wood and he owned her local newsagent. She kept hassling him, saying things like she'd buy her papers from another shop, until he agreed to come down and watch me. I remember the time that one of the other players said, 'there's that scout for United' and I started to try my best. In the end, I got a week's trial for United at Christmas.**

Wood, having worked for the club for 30 years, has become one of the chief stewards at Manchester United. He remembers well the day he discovered Ryan Giggs for United. "I went around watching junior football a lot in those days," he says. "I got some information that there was this player playing for Deans, and that I should have a look at him. So I did – I watched him home and away, and I liked what I saw. His pace, his balance, his general football knowledge, the way he caressed the ball and his shooting. He had everything. You felt that something was going to happen every time he got the ball. He was the sort of player who could turn a game round, even when his side were losing, and he did so several times as I watched him.

"So when I next was at the club, I passed the information on to Mr Ferguson who'd just arrived on the scene. I told him all about Ryan, and nothing happened for some time. Then I heard that he was connected with Manchester City although he wasn't tied to them by contract or anything like that. So I told the scouting staff here to follow it up, and again nothing happened. I had another word with Mr Ferguson and said: 'There's people knocking on this lad's door and if nothing happens we're going to lose him.' Then I got a telephone call on a Friday night from one of the United scouts, a guy named Allie Murphy. He asked about Ryan, and when and where we could see him play. We went down to the next six or seven games, but still things dragged on and on till I went to the boss and said: 'Look, we're going to have to do something about it,

otherwise another club will get him.' So the boss sent Brian Kidd down to look at him one Saturday. He got him on a week's trial and it just went from there."

Alex Ferguson takes up the story. "It was perhaps indicative of the state of our scouting system that Ryan Giggs didn't join us through normal club channels. I would have known nothing about Ryan until it was too late if it hadn't been for one of our stewards, Harold Wood. He came to me soon after I joined the club to ask if I had heard about Ryan Wilson, who was then playing for Salford Schools. Ryan later took his mother's name of Giggs, but he was Wilson in those days and the answer was no, we didn't know about him. I asked Brian Kidd, who was doing community work in football at that time, and he knew he was training with Manchester City. I told Joe Brown to get the lad down, and he arrived over the Christmas period."

**During my week's trial, I played against another team on trial for United and scored three in a 4–3 win. The other side gave me some gyp afterwards as I don't think I exactly enhanced their chances. I really enjoyed myself and liked everything I saw, but I thought that was it because I didn't hear anything else and continued training with City.**

Ferguson, however, had different ideas. "As soon as I saw him on the pitch," he remembers, "I knew he was a special footballer. We set out to make him a Manchester United player."

# football genius

# chapter three

There's no position on the football field as glamorous as that of the winger. There's something that sends a thrill down the spine at the very mention of the word. Of course football is about scoring goals, but the only thing that's comparable to seeing the ball hit the back of the net is seeing a winger leave a defender for dead with a shimmy of the hips and a sleight of foot to get a run on goal, or the space for a cross.

Back in the old days when teams employed two defenders and five attackers, each side had two specialist wingers. Their job was to wait for the ball on the flank, beat the defender and get a cross in, or occasionally run in on goal to score. Alf Ramsey changed all that when he realised that wingers were becoming obsolete in the days of four defenders, and he didn't have any good ones in his squad anyway. Geoff Hurst came into a new 4–4–3 formation in the middle of World Cup '66, and we all know what happened then. Ramsey was a fullback in his playing career, so maybe there was an element of revenge in his tactical reforms. Whatever the reason, it looked as if the winger was dead.

Thank God that wasn't the case. What evolved instead was the thoroughly modern winger who was able to switch into midfield at will, defend like the best of them and hit more than his fair tally of goals in the season. And, of course, outflank a fullback with his pace while showing off his moving-ball control like the best of the old boys. Ryan Giggs is very possibly the best modern winger the world has yet seen.

**The key to the game now is versatility. It's still about being different and getting the ball from the flank to the forwards, but there's more to it than that. You've got to add many more things to your game nowadays. You've got to do a lot more work than you used to, for example. You have to be able to defend. I had plenty of experience as a midfielder when I was younger so I don't find defending too difficult. I love tackling, for example. I'm not the strongest of tacklers, so the skill for me is timing it right. You've got to keep your eye on the ball.**

**To keep improving as a player, you have to profit from playing defensively. If you keep your eyes open you can learn to attack better from being forced to defend. I don't really like facing wingers myself. They cut the sort of figure that strikes fear into your heart. But if I find it incredibly difficult to defend against something a winger does, I'll bear it in mind to try it out later on someone else.**

Giggs can defend, for sure, but that's not why people rave about him. Since the first season he pulled on a United shirt, he has got the fans going thanks to his ability to tear at the wounded heart of opposing defences. In the early days, however, he was a little too ambitious and raw.

**When I first came into the team I just wanted to get the ball and beat the defender. The result of that is that the defender can read you. He'll think, 'oh he's just going to do that', and he'll be waiting for it. So you've got to have different options up your sleeve. You learn things over the years, and the more experienced you get, the more options you've got. When you're faced with a one-on-one, for example, you can run outside the defender, or run inside them, or not even attempt to take them on – just set somebody else up by passing them the ball. All these options are running around in your mind, but you've got to be positive and choose one of them quickly. If you dither about, you'll lose the ball. You've just got to be positive.**

It's not as simple as just instinctively getting past your man without thinking about it. It varies a lot, actually. Sometimes you can sense that a good chance is on the cards and you're given a bit of time to think about what you are doing and where you are moving to. This happened to me against QPR in 1994, when I scored after dribbling the ball on a long run. But in other instances the action happens so fast that you don't have time to think and you do just do something completely instinctively.

When it comes to running at defenders, there's no better feeling in football than taking on a defender and beating them – apart maybe from scoring a goal. You've got to be patient. I might try to beat a defender 10 times in a game, get tackled the first nine, then get past them the 10th, and go on to score a goal, or set one up. Actually, setting up a goal gives me just as much pleasure as scoring, because football is all about team work.

I'm often singled out for special treatment by the opposition; for instance, it's rare that I don't have a marker put on me. But when you're fit and playing well, it is great to realise it doesn't matter who's marking you, if you get the ball you're going to beat them. Obviously there are times when, if you're not playing so well and you're being closely marked, and you start to get frustrated. But then you've got to use your head and bring other players into play. Run your marker away and make space for others. The perfect example of this is probably Eric Cantona. Teams last year and the year before tried to man-mark him and he turned it to our advantage. He actually relished being man-marked.

Then there are the times when you have to put up with being marked by two players. Especially at Old Trafford... there are teams that come and they all pull back behind and try to stop you, so you have to beat two men before you get any space. It can be frustrating, but it necessarily creates space for other players, so you have to look for them making runs and get the ball to them.

There are no bad defenders in the Premiership. They simply wouldn't have got as far as they have got if they weren't brilliant players. But some players stand out and are always very tough opponents. Gary Kelly of Leeds and Liverpool's Rob Jones are lightning fast, for example, and get more experienced every game. Experience is a crucial factor – it gains defenders a good deal of time. Some older defenders have lost a yard of pace but can make up for that with their positional sense. I find defenders most difficult when they have a blend of speed and experience. Earl Barrett is a prime example. He's the sort of guy who gives you the least space and the most trouble.

Each defender you play is different from the one you faced the week before, so you've got to get to know their strengths and weaknesses. If you notice a weakness during the game you try and exploit it. By now, I know most of the defenders in the Premiership, so I know what to expect from them before the game begins.

Part of my job is to make a monkey out of defenders, which often leaves them feeling rather aggrieved. You do get fullbacks who try to intimidate you, saying how hard they are and how many lumps they're going to kick out of you. But I'm used to that now, and it's getting better every season. I used to get a lot more intimidation from defenders. When you're a young lad coming into the team, especially if you're a forward, you know that players are going to try and put you off your game. Either by talking to you throughout a game and telling you they're going to do this or that to you, or maybe just being physical with you. You've just got to feel that you're strong and overcome it. I suppose I've had more than my fair share of fouls, but it's inevitable really. The game is so quick nowadays that it's bound to happen.

When I was younger, I always played with boys older than me, so I was used to people trying to bully me out of it. When players start threatening me, I take it as a compliment. It shows they are wary about what I can do with the ball. Besides, there are few more pleasurable experiences on a football field than taking the mick out of defenders who have a go at you. I love that feeling of knocking the ball past a defender and keeping going. Just as he thinks he'll get a tackle in, you touch it a little bit more and you're away.

Giggs likes making a monkey out of goalkeepers, too, and is one of the players United depend on to get their goals. Like all goalscorers, he loves it. Like most, he can't quite explain what it feels like.

Scoring is a mixture of relief and joy. I'm always asked what it feels like and I've never been able to put that feeling into words. You're running so high on adrenaline, you're not thinking rationally. I don't tend to celebrate goals in a big way, although if it's important I won't be able to stop myself. Some players work out their routines before a match – Ian Wright of Arsenal must lose sleep wondering where to get the next one from. I just do what comes into my head. If we're three or four up and I score, a smile is usually enough.

The better the goals, the better the celebrations. The best goal I scored was against Tottenham a while back. I picked up the ball deep, ran past quite a few defenders and put the ball in the net. It was a great feeling, because it was a great goal. But it wasn't that important an occasion. I was

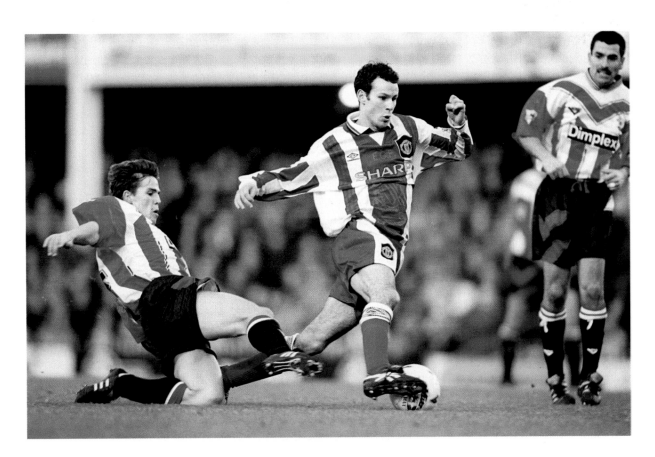

elated when I scored against Blackburn with a free kick in the last-but-one game of the season in 1994. We'd already won the League and the whole match was one big celebration. I didn't think it would get near the goal post, let alone go in the net. I went wild. It was a similar when I scored against Middlesbrough on the last day of the 1995/96 season. We needed to win to be sure of the League and we were already 2–0 up when I scored. That was the icing on the cake, really; it was the climax of a long, hard season.

My goalscoring was helped by Eric Harrison, the Youth team coach here. When I played in the Manchester United Youth team, he made me play as a centre forward, just to get me used to the different position. It added something new to my game. You'll find that generally with the United team, actually; all the players can play in a lot of different positions, which makes our game more fluid.

Anyway, when I was an apprentice, I used to really respect Gary Lineker. Everyone around me used to say, 'watch Lineker and learn'. He was the best. I used to study the way he got into the box at the right time; the way he judged his runs. He was brilliant at coming to the ball, checking and then getting behind defenders on their shoulders. The thing about him and Ian Rush is that they can be rubbish all game, do nothing, then get one chance and score. I still miss far too many, unfortunately, but the experience certainly sharpened me up.

I'm also one of the penalty specialists on the side. We've got a plastic wall at the training ground and a few of us will stay behind after training to practice our free kicks. Denis Irwin, David Beckham and I all try to whip it over the wall. It can add two or three goals to your tally every season. When it comes to deciding who's going to take each penalty, we just decide whereabouts the ball is and who fancies taking it. If it's on the right I'll take it more often than not, because I can bend the ball round the wall with my left foot and put the keeper in difficulty. The important thing is to get it on target – that's what the Boss always tells us. If it hits the post or the bar or the keeper saves it, you'll often get a chance off the rebound. And if the keeper has to touch it over the bar or round the post, you'll get a corner. So the important thing is to concentrate on hitting the target.

As for corners, I usually take the ones from the left, and I have four or five different options. The main two choices are simply putting it to the near post or putting it to the far post. You just look up and see where the players are positioned. We've got no set positions for corners, and I don't make any arm gestures or anything to explain what I'm going to do. I just see where the big guys are and where they're running to. We don't practice corners at Manchester United. We improvise.

I take corners from the right because I'm left-footed, but I'm not really that left-footed. My right foot isn't nearly as good as my left, but that doesn't mean it isn't any good. I think I can cross just as well with my right foot as my left. It's just that my shooting's not as good. It isn't as powerful, and it isn't as accurate. Defenders obviously know I'm left-footed, and often try to move me on to my right foot, but it doesn't bother me. I just go down the right and make sure I put a good cross in. I've practised a lot with my right foot, to make it better.

One of my role models when I was a kid, an opponent I still play against in the Premiership, was John Barnes. He's left-footed too. I'd watch him and try to copy him – the way he beat players, crossed and scored goals. I still rate him although he's slowed down. His passes rarely go astray, and that

has always been the case. What set him apart from other wingers was this ability to pass the ball, something I've really tried to take on board myself.

Indeed, Ferguson has recently taken to playing Giggs, the thoroughly modern winger, in a central midfield position if the need arises.

There was one game in the 1995/96 season when Roy Keane got sent off and the Boss asked me to drop back into midfield. I had one of the best games of the season. I'd played a bit in the middle when I was a kid, so I was used to it. Then there was another point in the season when we were playing Paul Scholes and Andy Cole up front, so there was no room for me on the wing and I had to drop back into midfield again. I really enjoyed it. You see a lot more of the ball, you work a lot harder, you generally get more involved. If you're on the wing you've got just one person to beat, sometimes two. When you're in the midfield there's a lot more variety. And you've got to be more responsible – if you lose the ball the results can be disastrous.

Ferguson trusted the Welshman, and needless to say there were no disasters. Giggs rarely lost the ball: the thoroughly modern winger showed the world that he had another string to his already impressive bow.

# fergie's first fledgling

# chapter four

Ryan Giggs was sitting at home watching the nine o'clock news with his mother on the evening of his 14th birthday when there was a knock on the door. They wondered who it could be. His mother went to answer.

**I couldn't believe it when Alex Ferguson walked into the room. He went off into the kitchen to talk to my mum. After he left, Mum came in and said that Mr Ferguson wanted to know if I'd play for United. There was never any doubt in my mind. I was United daft. By this time, I thought that nothing was going to happen for me at United, so I was incredibly surprised. It was a fantastic birthday present. I spent the rest of the evening on the phone to my mates and family, and didn't get a wink of sleep that night.**

Ferguson hadn't wasted much time recruiting Giggs. Clubs aren't allowed to sign young players until they have turned 14 years of age. It has to be on schoolboy forms, with an eye to two years further apprenticeship from the age of 16. This was one player Ferguson didn't want to let slip through the net. When he heard the news, Dennis Schofield wasn't very happy. "I was very disappointed when he signed for Manchester United," says the Manchester City scout. "Chief scout Ken Barnes had shaken hands with Ryan's father, and there was an agreement that he would sign for City when he became 14. City were undoubtedly going to sign him, but United got in there first. I wouldn't like to pin the blame on anybody in particular, I think it was a mixture of factors. The lad himself was a United fan, so that would have influenced him. Then you have to ask whether the manager at City knew about the player. I only ever dealt with the youth development officer and Ken Barnes, the chief scout, so I've no idea if the first team coaches were aware of him."

**I started playing for the A and B team at the weekend and trained with the squad for a week during the school holidays. Suddenly I was amongst hugely talented footballers. Bolton's Alan Thompson was there, and a young kid called Nick Barmby. The best player of the lot was called Raphael Burke. He was brilliant, but somehow never made the grade.**

Brian Kidd

Eric Harrison

Brian Kidd, now Ferguson's right-hand man at United, was keeping close tabs on the young player. "I was still only part-time when Ryan came on his first course at United," he says, "but even then it was so obvious that this was a lad with outstanding talent. It wasn't even a case of having to persuade anybody how good he was – his brilliance was there for all to see. It's very pleasing for all of us at United to see how his career has turned out. Ryan is a lovely lad and deserves every bit of his success."

Nicky Barmby also played in the England Schoolboy team, of which Giggs, though fiercely proud of being Welsh, was captain.

**Out of my nine matches as captain, we won seven, including victories over Germany, Holland, France and Belgium. I'm often asked why I played for England Schoolboys and went on to represent Wales at international level. When I played for Salford Juniors, they put forward two or three names every year for England Schoolboys. I went to the trials and did well and got into the team. But it wasn't an England team – it was an England Schoolboys' team, comprised of people who went to school in England. So I couldn't have played for Wales Schoolboys if I wanted to.**

**I also started playing for the Manchester United Youth team while I was still at school, though I was two years younger than most of the others. The Youth team is really designed for second year apprentices, but you sometimes get a lad who's still a schoolboy playing. So I played in three Youth Cups in a row. In my first year we got to the semi finals of the competition, but lost to Sheffield Wednesday. In my first apprentice year, we lost out to Tottenham Hotspur, again in the semis. In my second year as an apprentice, I was appointed captain and we got to the final and won the thing. By then, I'd started playing in the Reserves.**

**By the time I finally signed as an apprentice, after leaving school at the age of 16, it was a lot easier for me than other players of my age. I'd been there so often in the last couple of years I knew the place back to front. The main difference, though, was in the quality of training, and the fact that we suddenly went full time.**

When Giggs first started at United, Nobby Stiles was helping to coach the Youth team. "Ryan was very talented, very confident, a terrific lad and a pleasure to work with," says Stiles, in a statement as brief as one of his infamous tackles. Youth team coach Eric Harrison was delighted to have Giggs under his wing. "Before he came to the club I'd seen him play for Salford Juniors, and when he arrived here he was already an outstanding talent for such a young lad," he says. "I realised immediately that he could become a top player. He had tremendous speed and balance, he was very good with the ball, and he had the ability to change direction at pace. He was an outstanding prospect."

Harrison decided that Giggs needed a bit of working on, however. "The first thing I did with him was to change his position," he continues. "He had been playing as an out-and-out left winger, but I wanted him to play as a striker so that he could learn more about the game. I especially wanted to develop his running off the ball, an aspect of his game which was poor. Wingers can go ten minutes in a match without even touching the ball, but I wanted Ryan to be involved. So we played him as a striker and in training sessions he worked on the skills a striker needs. Ryan was happy to go along with the switch when we explained that it would improve his all-round game. We worked on his heading, too, and he gets the odd goal now with his head. Nowadays, of course, he's a brilliant winger but he's also a brilliant striker. He can play down the middle and, in my opinion, that's where he'll end up."

It wasn't all plain sailing for the young Giggs, who had to do his share of hard graft in the traditional manner of an apprentice.

**You get given certain jobs, like cleaning the corridors. I used to have to clean up the dressing rooms. It wasn't very nice at the time because you could see all the first-team players go off at 12.30 and you had to stay around until 4.30 tidying up the training ground. And you start thinking 'I wish I was in the Reserves, I wish I was a pro.' But you just have to wait. It was hard at the time, but in the end you have to appreciate it.**

**I got £29.50 a week plus £10 expenses. It doesn't seem much now, but believe it or not it was much more than I was used to. And it went up a fiver when I was 17. They really trained us hard, morning and afternoon. But I found everyone very welcoming, including the senior players. I remember the first senior player I spoke to was Viv Anderson. I played in a practice game against the first team, and I was up against him, so he chatted to me, telling me to slow down. He was probably just knackered, looking back.**

Harrison reckons that Giggs hasn't changed much since his days in the Youth team. "The biggest thing with Ryan," he says, "is that he's the same kind-hearted, level-headed lad he was when he first arrived. He's confident and realises he has great talent, but he's not at all arrogant or big-headed. I still love to watch him. He still loves to take people on – that's something we never tried to take away from him – and he's a great entertainer."

Around this time, Ryan Wilson became Ryan Giggs.

When I left school I made a decision to call myself Giggs. My mum and dad had split up by then and my mum remarried. My mum's side of the family had been brilliant in my upbringing and I wanted the world to know I was my mother's son.

For most of the 1990/91 season, when I was a second-year apprentice, I played for the Reserves and the Youth team. The first team seemed a long way off. Then one Friday, Brian Kidd came into the apprentice dressing room and said 'you're training with us today.' I couldn't believe it. So off I went with the likes of Robson and Hughes, whom I'd only just taken down from my bedroom wall.

Then I made the squad for a midweek away fixture at Bramall Lane against Sheffield United. I didn't think I'd be playing, and I was right. But it was a great experience. I remember I was sharing a room with Darren Ferguson – he got picked and went on as substitute.

Then the following Saturday I was named again. I thought it was just for the experience. We were playing Everton at home. Les Sealey came down and I remember him saying, 'I've just seen the team and you're sub'. The manager names the team during his team-talk an hour and a half before kick-off. He read out the names and sure enough, mine was down as sub. Strangely enough, I wasn't nervous – I'm hardly ever nervous before matches, and I didn't have enough time for anything to sink in. I came on in the first half when Denis Irwin got injured. I don't remember much about it now, funnily enough. I remember beating a few players and the crowd roaring my name, and feeling goose pimples. But it was all over in a flash.

Everton defender Kevin Ratcliffe remembers Giggs' debut well, although he wasn't too over-awed by his young compatriot that afternoon. "He showed a bit of pace, but he seemed very fragile, although it was too early really to judge him," he says.

Youth team coach Harrison continues: "I was absolutely delighted when Ryan made his first-team debut. He'd hardly played any matches for the Reserves, so he virtually jumped from the Youth team to the first team."

Giggs had to wait another two months before he got his next sniff of the first team. He felt completely out of the reckoning as the whole city started gearing up for the local derby at Old Trafford against Manchester City.

I was back with the Youth team and Reserves, and feeling a bit down. I remember a few of the players coming down and saying 'you're sub, you're sub'. I hadn't been involved so I was a bit surprised. I went into the changing room an hour and a half before the game to hear the team-talk and the boss started naming the side. I can always remember him saying: 'Ryan, you're playing on the left.' My hands just started shaking. Like I said, I didn't usually get nervous before matches, but it seems I made an exception for this one.

If it was a good time for Giggs to play his first full game for United, it was an even better one to score his first goal for the club, in a 1–0 victory. Or sort of score.

It was a real old goalmouth scramble. It hit me, then I think it hit someone else. Then it hit Colin Hendry, and then it went in. It was an own goal, truth be told, but Hendry didn't want his name against it. So, as it was my debut, the boss told the press I'd got it.

Typical Ferguson. Giggs, for a brief few days, was the toast of the red half of town. He was substituted by Mal Donaghy late in the game and didn't play again that season, but it didn't really matter in the Giggs household. Thanks to a canny bit of management by Alex Ferguson, the lad had a derby-winning goal under his belt.

# chapter five

Try and name a Great Britain XI and there is only one non-English player who definitely gets into the team. Ryan Giggs. Naturally Giggs, who was born in Cardiff, is one of the first players on the Welsh teamsheet. The fact that Giggs has a soft-spoken Manchester accent and once captained England Schoolboys has left many English fans thinking 'if only'. The same fans often presume that Giggs, looking at the relative success of the English team as opposed to that of the Welsh, will be thinking the same thing. Not at all. When he speaks about his country, you can see from his eyes that he really means it.

**I'm Welsh through and through. I was born in Wales, so were my mum and dad and my grandparents. I have never thought of playing for England and would never consider playing for England. I was brought up to be Welsh. I was born in Cardiff and spent my early years there. Even when I moved to Manchester, I regularly went back there. A lot of people ask me: 'Wouldn't you like to play for England? And I ask them: 'Would you like to play for Wales?' And they say: 'No, because I'm English.' So I say: 'Well it's because I'm Welsh.'**

**Apparently, before I started playing internationals, Terry Venables said to the Boss that he couldn't believe I was allowed to slip through the English net and play for Wales. It's flattering, but there was never any question of my playing for England. To be fair to the Boss, even though he's not exactly one to go out of his way to help the English cause, he did once take me into his office and say I'd have a better chance of playing in the World Cup if I made myself available for selection to England. But if I was going to be lucky enough to play for a country, it had to be Wales.**

Giggs sealed his Welsh footballing nationality by playing in an Under-18 match. Ironically, this was against England at Wrexham in the World Youth Cup in 1991. Jimmy Shoulder, the Director of Coaching for Wales who is also in charge of the Youth team, remembers the match well. "The English team were frightened to death by Ryan. They were talking about him as the best player of his age in Europe. He was the outstanding player on the pitch, even though England had a very strong team which included Barmby, Unsworth, Watson of Newcastle, Howe of Forest and Bart-Williams," he says. "In the return leg at Yeovil, I remember sitting in the dug-out with Terry Yorath. England were double-marking him. He got the ball right in front of us and was immediately ambushed by three players, but he got out of it as quick as a flash with a drag back and a couple of dummies. The England defenders were almost tackling each other as he ran off with the ball. Terry turned to me, shook his head and said: 'How the hell did he do that?'"

Shoulder maintains that Giggs couldn't even have played for England if he wanted to. "It's a complete red herring that he could have played for England," he says. "He was born in Wales, his parents are Welsh, so he is Welsh and simply doesn't qualify for England." Whatever the case, it seems that there was no doubt in Giggs' mind from the start.

**Now I'm incredibly proud when I put on that Welsh shirt. I don't sing the anthem before matches quite as well as my mum, but I know the words, despite what my mates reckon. We were taught them at school in Wales and my granddad was forever drumming them into me. I can't say anything else in Welsh though, apart from the odd word such as 'hello' and 'goodbye'.**

Welsh manager Terry Yorath gave Giggs his first taste of international football when he put the winger on the bench for the vital European Championship qualifier against West Germany on 16 October 1991. "I could have played him earlier than I did," says Yorath. "I was under tremendous pressure from the Welsh FA Committee to play him and from Alex Ferguson not to play him. When I gave him his debut, it turned out he was the youngest player ever to appear for Wales though that wasn't a record we had planned to beat – it just happened that way. But it's a record he deserves." Giggs came on with four minutes remaining and Wales 4-1 down.

**I didn't feel overawed at all, funnily enough. We were getting beaten and I was sitting on the bench dying to get on so I could try and change things. I only managed to get about three touches of the ball though. The Germans were incredible that day – the way they kept hold of the ball, and hardly let us get a touch.**

"He didn't show any nerves at all," remembers Yorath. "He was very quiet before the game, but he's a quiet lad. I had no worries about him and I felt it was the right time to give him his debut. He turned up to the training session and didn't look out of place at all, even though we had top players like Hughes, Rush and Saunders in the squad. But he could play with any group of players and look comfortable.

"Alex did put pressure on me not to pick him. I had a lot of phone calls from him and he made it perfectly clear he wasn't happy. He said Ryan didn't need the extra pressure of becoming an international at such a young age. I never experienced that sort of pressure from another manager, but I could understand his point of view. I also had to think of what was

good for Wales, and I felt the time was right to play him."

West Germany went on to pip Wales in the qualifiers, making it another case of so near but yet so far for the boys in red who'd fought an otherwise brilliant campaign.

Almost 18 months passed before Giggs made his full debut – by which time he'd established himself as a household name both in England and Wales. Yorath had eased him on to the international scene by naming him in the squad and bringing him on as substitute five times. "At the end of 1992 we played Belgium away and Ryan came on for the last half hour," says Yorath. "He looked ordinary and I told him: 'Now you know it isn't so easy.' He took in what I said because a few months later I gave him his first start in the return match and he was tremendous."

The return against Belgium was another crucial match – this time a World Cup qualifier – at Cardiff Arms Park. Giggs rewarded the Welsh fans for their boisterous support with an incredible goal.

**The goal against Belgium is one of my favourite goals of all time. We weren't really expecting to win because Belgium were a good team then. I volunteered to take a free kick outside the box. I just bent it over the wall and it went in. What made it better was that my family was there. Sometimes a few of them come up to Old Trafford, but not the whole lot of them. That day there were about 12 or 13. It makes you try harder, though you don't necessarily play better. I did that night, though. I played brilliantly – the best match I've ever played for Wales.**

**Funnily enough, I found it surprisingly easy to settle into the Welsh set-up. Ian Rush and Mark Hughes had been my heroes for as long as I could remember, but then I found out that they, and other older lads like Neville Southall, were also unbelievably welcoming. Kevin Ratcliffe said an amazing thing to the press when I made my debut: that he could now tell his grandchildren that he had played with Ryan Giggs. That sort of thing doesn't half make you feel relaxed.**

Ratcliffe, now manager of Chester City, remembers making the statement. "When I said it, it was a little bit tongue-in-cheek, but everybody knew he would be a big star right from his early days. Man United have always wanted somebody to emulate George Best – it was said of Norman Whiteside, although he wasn't a similar type of player at all. Ryan is a player more along those lines than anyone else they've had. He's very adaptable, and can play anywhere across the midfield or across the attack.

"I remember the game against Belgium particularly well, because I was making my comeback in international football after a gap of a couple of seasons," continues Ratcliffe. "It was an important match and we were under a lot of pressure. Ryan was very quiet; he generally does his

own thing and doesn't live up to the 'superstar' tag at all. He's very level-headed. I think I was more nervous than he was, because I'd been out for a long time and I was a Third Division player."

The atmosphere in Cardiff Arms Park that night was just brilliant. The lads who'd been in the squad for some time – who played when Wales used to turn out at Wrexham and Ninian Park – said the reception the players received from the crowd was almost like having a goal start. When I scored you could have heard the noise at Wembley.

The win against Belgium set up Wales for a place in the Finals. On 17 November 1993, Wales had to beat Romania by two clear goals to qualify for the final stages of the tournament. We had a well-balanced side with young players like Gary Speed and myself, as well as old heads like Saunders, Hughes, Rush and Southall. I reckon we had a good chance of doing well in America. The match started badly when they scored through Hagi. That really got us going. We started attacking like mad, trying to equalise. We got one back through Dean Saunders and then missed chance after chance. When things are going well for them, the Romanians are untouchable. But the moment things go wrong, their heads go down.

As soon as we equalised and started to get on top, Hagi went on to the wing and sulked. You could see he just didn't want the ball. I've never seen anything like it; a player of his genius disappearing, when qualifying for the World Cup hinged on the result. I thought we would do it then, especially when we got a penalty, but Paul Bodin missed. If we had scored the penalty we would have got another goal or two, I'm sure of it, because we were all over them. After the penalty I had half a chance. I got put through and only had the keeper to beat, but the defender came across and blocked it. Then as we piled forward, they got a breakaway and that was it. Raducioiu scored a second for Romania, and Wales were out of the World Cup.

When we came off the pitch, we were really dejected. The dressing room was silent afterwards, nobody was talking. I'd never felt lower, and I was better off than some. There were lads in there who had given everything for years to Wales and they knew their chance had gone. Terry Yorath was brilliant that night. He said to us all: 'Listen, it was the best you could do. We came so close.'

Realistically, it was the best chance we had for years and we'd blown it. I was in a terrible mood afterwards. I'm a terrible loser. If we lose I'll be in a bad mood for days, not just for hours. I'm really competitive. Ever since I've been a kid I've had a will to win. I hate losing at cards or Trivial Pursuit – I'll cheat if necessary – so you can imagine what it was like not getting to the World Cup Finals. It was the worst moment of my football career, along with Leeds beating us to the Championship in 1992.

The game against Romania was to be the last match Terry Yorath managed for Wales. His contract was up for renewal at the end of the year and he intimated that the Welsh Football Association should pay him more money for his services. The Association simply didn't renew Yorath's contract when the time came. It is a move that still angers Giggs.

I always got on well with Terry. All the lads respected him because he was former Welsh international and a fine manager. Once he got everything sorted out we started playing really well. He had a good laugh with the lads and treated us like adults. Peter Shreeves took the training and he was brilliant. Then after all his hard work, Terry was allowed to go. Immediately after the World Cup campaign, when he had done so much, he was kicked out. It seems to me that something

**should have been done to allow him to stay as manager, especially as his son had died less than a year before he was released. We couldn't believe it. Everyone wanted him to stay. We had nearly got into the World Cup, we had quite a young team and it looked like we could build a serious challenge for the European Championship. Instead, Terry wasn't kept on and it upset the whole balance.**

Several months later, John Toshack was appointed technical director – a strange move, as Toshack was still working for Real Sociedad and had just signed a new contract for the Spanish club. Toshack only lasted one match – a friendly 3–1 home defeat by Norway in which Giggs didn't play – before jumping ship. At this point Mike Smith, Toshack's number two (and an Englishman), was appointed caretaker manager – an unenviable task in a difficult political climate. Smith had a couple of friendlies before Wales launched into their European Championship qualifiers. Their group included Germany, Bulgaria, Moldova and Georgia. Wales started off well enough, with a 2–0 win in Albania where Giggs scored the second goal, but then their campaign came off the rails with defeats in Moldova (3–2) and Georgia (5–0).

**The draw for the 1996 European Championship was never going to make life easy for us. We did well against Germany, but apart from that it was disappointing. I was injured that season and I only played in two matches in the qualifiers. I couldn't believe that 5–0 defeat at Georgia. It must be the worst defeat we've ever had. I was watching the score on Teletext, and the goals just kept going in.**

Smith didn't have much time to assess Giggs' potential, but he liked what he saw. "He is one of the true talents, a player who would be in the team if you were picking a Great Britain side. He has awesome pace and, just as importantly, he is extremely perceptive. The way he and Eric Cantona combine, for example, is almost uncanny at times. For Wales, he loves playing off Mark Hughes, whose great strength is holding the ball up and laying it off.

"Ryan has a bit of an aura about him. Defenders know he is capable of producing something special either through his pace or with a little trick if they go close to him. His temperament is superb – like all top performers he is 'cold' before the game, unaffected by the occasion. He will perform whatever the level of pressure on the players."

Smith was finally fired after Wales lost 1–0 at home to Georgia on 7 June 1995 and Bobby Gould, an Englishman who won the FA Cup with Wimbledon in 1988, was appointed in his place.

**When you look at what Jack Charlton did for Ireland, you've got to come to the conclusion that it doesn't matter what nationality the manager is. All the players like and respect Bobby and there is a feeling of optimism about the World Cup qualifiers. You've always got a chance. I'm used to winning things with Man United, so I don't see why I can't win with Wales. It's every boy's dream to play in the World Cup Finals, and I'm no different really.**

Smith is upbeat about Wales' chances of qualification, especially with Giggs around. "He is very important to Wales' hopes of qualifying for the World Cup. You really see a difference in the side when he's playing. There's no doubt he has it within him to become one of the all-time greats." And his determination might be a key factor in the equation. "I think he is intent on seeing Wales qualify for the World Cup in France. It was a great tragedy that George Best, for example, never played in the Finals, but that stage is demanded for a player with the talent of Ryan Giggs. At Euro '96 it was the isolated moments – that chip by Poborsky, for example – that live in the memory, and Ryan is the type of player capable of producing those memorable moments."

**I love playing for my country. Every match is a huge event – you have five or six days' preparation just for that 90 minutes. The games themselves are hugely exciting to play. There's much more tension than in Premiership matches, because you're playing for your country and so are the players on the other side, and everybody is that much more determined. It's not often you get the chance to do something for your country, so you've got to make the most of it. It makes me enormously proud, even more so than playing for Manchester United.**

first two seasons:

# 1991/92 & 1992/93

## chapter six

Having tasted the atmosphere of a local derby – and scored the winning goal to boot – the end of the 1989/90 season saw Ryan Giggs thirsty for more top flight action with Manchester United. But even though the 17 year old had impressed in his opening games, there were two things that stood between himself and a regular place on the wing for United's first team. They were called Andrei Kanchelskis and, more particularly, Lee Sharpe.

**Sharpe was playing so well – he'd just been made Young Player of the Year – that I really thought I'd have to wait a couple of years before I became a regular in the team. I didn't bear a grudge or anything; we were always good friends. I simply thought I'd have to sit things out a little. In the end Sharpey had some injury problems, so 1991/92 became my first full season with the club.**

United fans had every reason to look forward to the new season in the summer of 1991. They had followed their 1990 Wembley triumph over Crystal Palace in the FA Cup with an impressive run in the European Cup Winners' Cup which saw them get to the Final, in Rotterdam, against Johan Cruyff's Barcelona. What's more, they had put in a cracking performance and confounded most tipsters by winning the game 2–1. But however proud the win had made the red side of Manchester, there was still one trophy they had failed, again, to lift. United hadn't won the League Championship for a quarter of a decade and everybody was letting them know about it. It was a statistic that was to come to obsess Giggs too, although at the time it wasn't the first thing on his mind.

**At the start of the 1991/92 season I'd played just two League games for United, but already I was starting to get stopped in street. It was impossible to escape the fact that it was 25 years since United had last won the title back in 1967, in the days of Best, Law and Charlton. Everywhere you went people reminded you of it, the media was full of it, fans would come to you in the street and say they hoped the wait was over. It didn't really affect me, though. It wasn't a big problem in my mind. I'd just come into the team, I was 18 and all I wanted to do was play for Manchester United.**

Although he didn't make United's opening line-up, at home to Notts County, Giggs was substitute and came on for his friend Darren Ferguson in the second half. A week later, away at Everton, he was named as number 11 in the side. It was the first of 15 consecutive matches in the team, who were flying high at the top of the table. Ryan scored three goals. Of course, with United at the top of the table again and a good-looking young number 11 flashing his skills round the country, the George Best comparisons started.

**The manager told me to ignore them and just to get on with my game, so that's what I did. I can't say it wasn't flattering, but I didn't want to be a flash in the pan, so I concentrated on learning as much as I could about first-team football.**

He had plenty of chances to acquaint himself with life at the top of the domestic football pile. He made 38 appearances that season. He hadn't quite made the number 11 shirt his own – he also wore the numbers 2, 4, 5, 7, 9 and 10 as well as the substitutes jerseys that term – but he had made himself an almost automatic entry on the team-sheet.

**I can't really say when it sunk in that I was a regular United player. It all seemed to happen so fast. Looking back, what was on my mind had suddenly shifted from what I could do to get into the team to what I could do to stay there.**

After early exits from the FA and Cup Winners' Cup, the season saw United battling on two fronts: the League and the League Cup (or Rumbelows Cup as it was then known). United got to the final of the latter competition, thanks in part to a vital semi final goal by the Welsh prodigy in a tough semi final against Middlesbrough, then beat Nottingham Forest in the final with a McClair goal.

**To play at Wembley and win a trophy in my first full season was beyond my wildest dreams. I'd played two games there before for England School-boys, and there's no place like it – though it's not actually my favourite ground and I've never had a really good game there for Man United. It's the dressing rooms, the roar of the crowd, the whole occasion really... it's so different from anywhere else you play. And that occasion was extra special because I passed to Brian McClair for the winner.**

The Rumbelows Cup was all very well, but it wasn't the trophy United most wanted that season. For a long time, it looked like they were going to end the jinx and lift the Championship as well, as Giggs recalls.

We'd signed Peter Schmeichel, Paul Parker and Andrei Kanchelskis and at first the season went like a dream. We started like a greyhound out of a trap and it was five games before Peter conceded his first goal. For almost the entire season we were top of the table. But that Easter we had a terrible fixture backlog and we blew it. We lost at home to Nottingham Forest with four matches to go, but the game that really did it for us was away at West Ham two days later when we lost 1–0. We knew we'd blown it. They had been rubbish all season, and suddenly they were brilliant against us.

Technically, it wasn't all over yet. On the second last day of the season Leeds were playing Sheffield United and we were playing away at Liverpool later that afternoon. Leeds won 3–2, which meant we had to win at Anfield. It's a terrible place to have to go and get a result. We lost 2–0 and the Liverpool fans really enjoyed us going down. They loved it, loved the fact that even though their team wasn't in the running, at least we weren't going to win the title.

It really hurt, blowing it in 1992. I'm a terrible loser. I hate losing at anything, no matter how trivial. If I have a bad game for United, it's the worst. I go into the dressing room and I'm always the last to get in the shower. I just sit there for half an hour, going over in my mind where it went wrong, where I could have made more of a contribution, working out how I missed that sitter. After the Liverpool game it was like when Wales got knocked out of the World Cup. No-one could say anything. It wasn't as bad for me as for the older players like Robbo and Brucey, though. They thought their chance had passed them by.

At Liverpool, when you come out of the changing rooms you have to walk about 20 or 30 yards to the coach. As I was walking towards the bus after that match, a bunch of Liverpool lads asked me for my autograph. I signed it for them and they just laughed and tore the pieces of paper up in my face. The manager always reminds me of that when we play Liverpool now, to wind me up... and it works.

I don't think I realised quite what winning the title meant to the fans until that summer. Whenever I went out in Manchester, everyone was saying 'what happened last year?' Everywhere you went,

1993 PFA Young Player of the Year

A stunning goal against Spurs, 19 September 1992

you could see how much it had hurt the fans. I think we all learnt from that and there was no way we weren't going to win it the following year. We felt a huge responsibility to those supporters. For a club like Man United, 26 years is a long time to go without winning the title – and with any luck the fans will never have to wait that long again. All that summer I couldn't stop thinking about it, how we'd lost to Leeds, and I couldn't wait for the next season to come. We could have thought 'oh no, we're never going to win it,' but in fact everyone's attitude was 'right, we'll show everyone this time round.'

The close season saw the European Championship in Sweden, but as Wales hadn't qualified, for Giggs it was a much-needed rest. But no amount of rest seemed to have done him or any of his team-mates much good in August 1992.

When the 1992/93 season started, at first it seemed like we were trying to show everyone how bad we were. We couldn't win a throw-in. After three games we were bottom of the table after away defeats at Sheffield United and Ipswich and an awful 3–0 home drubbing by Everton. Things picked up with a run of five wins, but it started to look like we were going to have to wait another year for the title.

Then in November Alex Ferguson bought Eric Cantona from Leeds. Before he arrived, I don't think any of us were aware of quite how good a player he was – apart from Brucey and Pally who'd raved about him when we'd played Leeds. I had no idea that he was the player that he is until he came to United. He's so easy to play with. You know that he has the ability to make a pass no one else could make, and when you make runs you just know you're going to get the ball right on your foot. People say he must be hard to play with because he's so unpredictable, but he's always the one working out what I'm trying to do, not the other way round. I've never played with a better player.

With Eric on board we believed in ourselves completely. We were determined it wasn't going to go the same way it had the previous year. The turning point was the home game against Sheffield Wednesday. The previous year, Easter had finished us off but this time – just when it looked as if our chance had gone again when we were losing 1–0 at home to Sheffield Wednesday – Brucey stepped up and scored the equaliser. Then, in so much injury time it was almost the next season by the time he did it, he headed the winner too. After that we knew it was our year.

After the right-to-the-wire finish of the previous season, United had things a little easier at the end of 1992/93. This time around their main challengers, Aston Villa, got the yips, and United cruised to victory. In the end, the margin at the top of the table was a fingernail-friendly 10 points.

When the title was finally won, we weren't even playing. Aston Villa had to play Oldham who were fighting relegation on the Sunday to keep their challenge going. The match was live on Sky and the Boss had banned us from watching it, but I went round to a mate's house and though I couldn't bear to watch the first half I sneaked a look at the second.

When Oldham won, we went mad. And as soon as we knew we'd won the title, Steve Bruce rang everyone and told them to come round to his house. So we all piled round and, even though we were playing Blackburn the next day, it was quite a party. We all felt this enormous relief that we'd done it, and we just wanted to congratulate each other; it was a family thing with all the wives and kids there. It was even more special, I think, for some of the players who'd been there for years, like Bryan Robson. I mean, after all that time he'd been at United, finally to win the title was fantastic. He went mental at the party, and he definitely wasn't the first to leave.

The next day we played Blackburn at home. The atmosphere was incredible; you could feel 26 years' weight lifting off 40,000 shoulders. But we hadn't had the standard preparation the night before and Blackburn were pretty determined to ruin the party. They went into an early lead, so I was pretty pleased (to say the least) to score the equaliser from a free-kick. We went on to win the match, and the atmosphere was out of this world when we went up to pick up our medals and our trophies.

I thought: 'This is as good as it can get.' Little did I know it was only just beginning.

**team-mates**

**chapter seven**

Peter Schmeichel is obviously a great keeper. He's just so big and awesome it's scary. I reckon that half the time, he saves the ball because he's frightened the opposing centre forward to death. I just call him Pete, though some of the lads call him Schmikes. He's exactly the same off the pitch as on it – he's very aggressive, and he shouts all the time. His English is very good and he's even developed a bit of a Manchester accent. He's a great guy, really. He always stays late after training to help us with shooting practice, and that even though Keaney blasts the ball straight at him from close range all the time to wind him up. He's also one of the people you can speak to if you need some advice because he's so experienced. Pete's a very superstitious guy – you'll see him kick the bottom of each goal post at the beginning of each half. Strangely enough, it usually seems to work.

Denis Irwin, the left back, is quite a funny person: he's very dry and quick-witted. He's the most consistent player in the club — we call him Mr Reliable. You need someone on the pitch who's going to get eight out of 10 every week, and that's Denis. He's also very good at free-kicks: he just blasts 'em.

We call him Maysie. He's definitely the loudest player in the team. He shouts when you're next to him as if you're on the other side of the room. He came from Blackburn, and for the first year he was very quiet. I know a few of the Blackburn players, and they'd say 'How's Maysie getting on?' and I'd say 'oh, he's all right, he's quiet ain't he though?' And they'd say '*What?*' And then these last few months he's lived up to his reputation, since he started getting more of a regular place in the team. He's always playing practical jokes and slaughtering people for what they're wearing.

Gary Pallister is universally known as Pally, although he has also been known as Dolly Day-dream and Crazy Legs. Pally's really funny. He's the Peter Pan of the team: he's 30, but he reckons he's still about 25. He used to have really appalling dress sense, but it's got a bit better recently because everybody ripped the mick so much. Pally's very loud. When we're training he's always moaning at Kiddo because he's gassed off that we're doing too much. 'We should be resting the players, we've got a game next week' – that sort of thing. He's dead lazy, he's always trying to get out of running. We'll be five minutes into our warm up and he'll come running in. He's always first at training, mind; it's just the running he hates.

Gary Neville is always getting the mick taken out of him because he's the most dedicated player in the team. He's always the first player to arrive at training and he's always the last to leave. He's always having discussions with Kiddo or asking the dietician questions about how he can improve his diet. But he's a great player to have in the side and he's made incredible progress, so maybe all the dedication has paid off. He's become an England international now so maybe we shouldn't really tease him, but we do.

Phil Neville has only just come into the team, so he's really quiet. I see Phil a lot off the pitch, and he's quite a good laugh. He's exactly the same as his brother in that he's very dedicated. It's incredible that he's got into the team so quickly. Phil and Gary's dad's called Neville Neville, which is pretty funny. Keaney's spreading a rumour that his grandad's called Neville Neville Neville. We know Neville Neville and he's been tremendous, though – he's a really nice guy.

Nicky Butt is probably my best friend off the pitch. He's great to have on the pitch, he's so tenacious and tough-tackling. He could turn out to be the new Bryan Robson. I went through the Youth team with him, so I've got to know him pretty well. He's really funny because he can't take a joke. If you take the mick out of him he'll lose his temper really quickly.

Becks, as David Beckham is known, is always getting the mick taken out of him because he's so flash. He's a typical Cockney – he's got this really strong London accent. When he wants you to kick the ball he yells ''It it'', which sounds really funny. Then when you get into the back of his car, he says: 'Don't scuff me levver.' We're always imitating him, but he doesn't mind. He just laughs. He always wears nice clothes and he's always got his hair slicked back, so he gets a lot of stick for being a pretty boy.

Eric's got more outgoing the longer he's stayed at the club. We all respect him because he's one of the best players in the world, and the club's fortunes have changed since he's come. He's a dream to play with: I've never come across such perfectly weighted passes. He knows exactly how fast we all run and puts the ball in exactly the place we can meet it. He's such a cool customer (he can wear anything and get away with it). And look at the way he takes penalties. He hasn't missed one for the club yet, and I don't think he ever will. He's not at all arrogant, though, as some people who don't know him make out. If you go out for a drink Eric's always there, and he's quite witty. He likes a joke. His English is better than he lets on. In fact, his English is perfect if he wants it to be. Sometimes he just doesn't want it to be.

**Brian McClair is probably the most intelligent player in the team. He's always telling jokes that none of the rest of us get. He's always talking about things that go above our heads, too. But Choccy is always someone you can go to if you've got a problem. He's quite quiet, but he's very dry. He's always moaning at Kiddo, too, for lying. We'll be running and Kiddo will say 'right, five left' and he'll mean five sets, or something like that, not just five minutes. Brian hates that.**

Roy Keane's probably the funniest person in the team. It doesn't matter who you are, he'll just have a go at you. He takes the mickey something chronic – he even slaughters Brian McClair. Him and Pally are always at each other, even though they're best friends off the pitch. In the changing room, Keanie'll say 'watch this' and he'll start humming or singing a song near Pally. Five minutes later Pally will be singing the same song. It never fails, that one.

Andy Cole's had to change the way he plays since he got here: he was much more of a lone striker at Newcastle, and now he's more part of the team. He's a very quiet lad when he's with the lads, but I room with him and he's not quiet when we're in our room. Once he gets hold of a Sony Playstation he has a riot.

Karel is a very exciting player and of course he was one of the top performers in Euro '96 – everybody must remember his goal at Villa Park against Portugal. Some people are saying that he's the new Kanchelskis, but he's a different kind of player from Andrei. He's the only one of the 1996 intake of players who didn't speak any English when he arrived, but he rooms with Choccy, which should be interesting for him. Come to think of it, Choccy probably speaks fluent Czech. Like a lot of Eastern European players, Karel is very strong and fit.

Jordi is the only one of the 1996/97 signings who I saw play before he came to join United. He impressed me – and the Boss – when he played for Barcelona in the Champions' League against Manchester United a couple of years before. Barcelona are huge, so he knows how to handle the pressures of playing for a top-class club. Jordi has a lovely technique and touch but I don't think he knows what his best position is. That in itself may be a good thing, because opponents won't immediately know how to handle him.

Paul Scholes, Scholesy, is a man of very few words. He's quite dry though. He's already proved himself as a goalscorer and he's going to get better. He's incredibly dedicated and incredibly accurate. Every shot he takes in training is on target – it's amazing. He never misses.

And Ryan Giggs? Ryan Giggs is quite a quiet guy, but he's always in there with a joke when the opportunity arises. He's a simple sort of lad with simple sorts of pleasures: his mates, the odd pint in the local pub, going down the city centre to buy some clothes; watching videos, playing pool. Oh, and he likes playing football a bit, too.

under pressure

# chapter eight

**Being a footballer is not just about training on weekdays and playing on a Saturday afternoon. It's about afterwards, too, and that's probably the hardest bit. In fact that's definitely the hardest bit. It can get really tough sometimes.**

Ryan Giggs hardly ever seems to get flustered. He's a cool, calm customer who rarely breaks out of a considered monotone in interviews about his football career. But when you ask him about his life off the pitch (in this case, the pressures of being a footballer), there's emotion in his voice and you see more of the real Giggs emerging. Being a footballer who is a household name may well seem like a bed of roses... but there are plenty of thorns to avoid. When Giggs started emerging on the scene, Alex Ferguson was well aware of the pressures a young footballer faced.

**When I was 17, I'd just come into the team and everyone wanted to speak to me, but the manager refused all the interviews. His line was, 'he's a young lad who's new in the team. I want him to concentrate on his football.' I was quite happy – I didn't want to do interviews anyway.**

**The trouble with some elements of the press is that if they can't find a story, they tend to start making one up. Everyone started thinking I was a special case and needed to be protected from the outside world to stop me becoming another George Best. They thought because I was a little like him on the pitch, I must be like him off it too. But I wasn't a special case. None of the young players at United are allowed to talk to the press and I reckon that's quite right. You're still a teenage kid; you're not a rock star who wants to be all over the papers, you're a young lad who wants to play football. Suddenly all these cameras, microphones and notebooks get shoved in your face and you say something daft or boring and you get crucified for it.**

Ferguson didn't want all the attention to go to Giggs' head and stop him from concentrating on his football. "My prime concern," explained the United manager, "was the clear risk of a repetition

84

of the George Best scenario from the Sixties or the Gazza syndrome of more recent times. I knew what I had to do; I bolted the Old Trafford door and made sure Ryan was safe inside. If we had allowed open house with Ryan, we would have been asking for a state of media anarchy. It would have been Bedlam. They would never have left him alone and I'm afraid he would have been exploited as an innocent victim of the media wars that are now part of our daily lives. I understand why he is such a magnet. There are not too many of his kind around, but that's not my problem. It doesn't mean we should step back and allow him to be turned into a commercial sideshow for the spin-off merchants.

"My firm intention is that he won't fall victim to that infamous trap of British sporting life: the toppling of our idols. They simply want to pull down the legend, break it apart and shatter the person inside. George Best was a prime example and one of the earliest to suffer for it as well."

The Best comparisons were the main worry for Ferguson, but they didn't bother Giggs. Ferguson didn't really have to worry too much as it happened – Giggs turned out to be the sort of player who doesn't let all the praise and attention go to his head.

**I never really took any notice. It never really came into my head. It was flattering, I suppose – it's nice for people to say things like that. The manager said to me it's bound to happen; you're a young lad playing on the left, wearing number 11. A lot of players have had it before, and I'm sure plenty will have it again in the future.**

**One of my main advantages is that I was brought up really near the ground, so when I started playing for the club I didn't have to uproot myself and start finding my feet. Some lads have to move miles from home and when they arrive they haven't got any mates or anyone they can trust, so it's quite easy to get into trouble. My family was all around me, so I didn't even need to leave home.**

And I already had a group of friends – mainly the lads I'd played football with at Deans – who I'd known for years, and who didn't change the way they behaved towards me when I became famous. They still take the mickey out of me all the time, which helps me keep my feet on the ground.

One of the problems of being a footballer is dealing with the public while you're trying to go about your daily life. One of the biggest chores is autograph hunters. Hundreds of them gather outside United's training ground, the Cliff, every day.

Once I broke into the first team at United, I started signing a few more autographs. When you join the club, it's made clear that you are representing Manchester United and you should behave accordingly. The Boss is also very clear that the people who want autographs are the people who give us our livelihood and that we owe them our time and our good manners. And that's absolutely right. We all try to sign as many as we can. That said, things can get out of hand. During school holidays, the Cliff gets overrun with people; thousands upon thousands turn up. My mum dropped me off there once just as an entire party of sightseers was getting off a coach. I had to say to Mum, 'put your foot down and get me in quick.'

The worst times are when you're out with a girlfriend or something having a meal. All you want is a quiet time, then suddenly somebody intrudes and all the attention's focused on you. Like everybody I have my good days and my bad days, and sometimes I don't take kindly to this intrusion. Especially if someone's rude. They sometimes come up to you and say 'autograph' and stick a piece of paper under your nose. And I look round and say: 'Please? Thank you?' I just can't see how people can be so rude.

If people are polite, I don't mind. You're bound to get people coming up to you when you're in a restaurant or a public place. But the worst thing is when you want to have a conversation with the

person you're with and someone you don't know comes up to you and wants to have a chat. They want to talk about the game last week, or about football – which at times is the last thing I want to talk about when I'm trying to relax.

Fans also try to contact me by post – I gets hundreds of letters every day, so many that I've employed my grandfather, a retired policeman, to deal with them all. It's mostly people looking for signed autographs, but you get some weird stuff – girls' underwear and teddy bears, loads of teddy bears. There's this one girl, she's from Japan, she keeps knitting me scarves and hats and stuff. The best things I get sent are tapes and CDs. Oh, and I get the odd proposal of marriage – mostly from seven year olds, though.

If it's not the public trying to contact Giggs, it's the press, who are more interested in his private life than he's interested in telling them about it.

It used to annoy me more than it does now, but it's still pretty bad. You can accept a reporter wanting to talk to you if you've had a good game, or even a bad game. It's when they want to talk to you about other things outside football that it gets hard, about girlfriends and your private life for example. It doesn't upset me so much any more. I just don't read the papers. If my friends find out about something they really take the mick. They say things like, 'Hey, do you see where you were when you were out with us the other night in Salford? You were in London, with a girl.' It really gets stupid sometimes. I had a haircut and it made front page. Can you imagine that happening to you? How annoying that would be? I don't see the big deal. I get sick of it, so I'm sure the public must get sick of it sometimes too.

As far as girlfriends are concerned, I can make one amazing revelation: I have them. But that's all I'm prepared to say. I prefer to keep my private life just that – private. And I am getting a little fed up with press photographers jumping into the cab every time I'm out with a girl, as if this is the most incredible news in the world. I also object to the way any girl who is linked with me gets photographers on her doorstep and her picture plastered all over the papers. I've grown sort of used to it, but they haven't and it's not really on.

Unfortunately, it makes having a personal life extremely difficult. Certainly the media interest in my relationship with Dani Behr was hard on us both. I first met Dani when she interviewed me for her programme Surf Potatoes. We chatted for about 15 minutes and got on really well. But that was it. Then we bumped into each other in Marbella when she was interviewing Sharpey for the same programme and we got chatting in a club that evening. The next day, we met up on the beach and ended up spending the next four days together. I called her up when I got back to England and we started seeing each other when we could at weekends. Because we were so high profile it made life difficult, especially when the papers got hold of it. Even the fans had their own opinions. Girls would come up to me and say, 'Why are you going out with that Dani Behr?' I think a lot of it was jealousy because she was so well known. The relationship was good while it lasted but it's all over now. We still talk, though, so we really are just good friends.

Another thing that really annoyed me was when, in 1993, a newspaper decided to dig into my family's private life. They can write what they like about me as a footballer, but when they start invading my family's privacy and twisting the truth, it's not on at all. I can see how Diego Maradona felt when he shot those reporters, but of course I'd never go that far. One reporter did go a little too far once, though. I was at my mum's house and he just kept knocking on the door. He wouldn't stop. So my stepdad answered the door and threw this minestrone soup all over him. He didn't knock again after that. He shouted 'You've scalded me! You've scalded me!' and that's the last we saw of him.

I know places I can go where I won't be bothered. Usually if I want to go out, I'll just go to a local pub with my mates where everybody knows me so they don't pester me. Or I'll just go to a mate's house where I won't be bothered. I can't go into Manchester city centre as much as I'd like – I have a bit of a weakness for clothes, and I'd love to be able to go shopping more often. But there are a few shops that know me, and some of them even open up specially for me.

The only place I can really escape the public attention is abroad. I tend to go to the United States, usually Florida, in the summer. It's brilliant, because I can actually forget I'm famous for a while and just walk around without anyone bothering me, if I avoid the touristy parts. Sometimes it's quite funny because someone looks you up and down really strangely but they can't place you because you're out of context, so they just walk off thinking: 'I'm sure I know that guy from somewhere.'

It's easy to get annoyed with the hassle of being a footballer, but it's such an enjoyable profession that you really don't dwell on the hassle much, especially once you've got used to it. You've just got to accept that with a team like Manchester United you'll always be in the spotlight. It's part and parcel of doing the only job I've ever wanted to do. Sure there are lows. But the highs are much higher. Much, much higher.

season three 1993/94

chapter nine

So what do you do over the summer when you're a 19-year-old lad who's just won his first Championship? Much the same as any other 19 year old, it seems.

**I went on holiday with my mates to Malta. It was great to relax knowing the title was in the bag, but I knew the boss wouldn't let us rest on our laurels and it would be back to hard work as soon as we got back to The Cliff. We weren't wrong. Pre-season training was its usual hell.**

Ferguson had good reason to work his troops hard. The last time United had won the League title, back in 1968, they'd followed it up by becoming the first English club to win the European Cup. Ferguson desperately wanted to emulate Sir Matt Busby's achievement.

Giggs' first European experience was a two-legged tie against Honved which United won at a canter, 3–2 away and 2–1 at Old Trafford. Then all that stood between them and a place in the round robin section of the tournament was another home-and-away contest against Turkish champions Galatasaray. The first leg was at Old Trafford and United seemed to have the tie sewn up in the first 13 minutes with two goals, the first from Bryan Robson and the second an own goal. Then United found that a City fan had written the matchscript.

**We got off to a great start at Old Trafford, and then we got casual. We took our foot off the pedal at 2–0 and then their striker scored a wonder goal from 35 yards. If that hadn't gone in we'd have won the tie because they weren't going to score at their place if the match had gone on all month. Then they scored two more quick goals and suddenly it was a disaster. It even looked that I'd be in the side that lost United's proud, unbeaten-at-home run in Europe. Luckily Eric scored to save us and earn a 3–3 draw, but it was stupid. We should have finished them off.**

**We had a chance to make amends in the return leg and we were fairly optimistic about the side**

winning the return in Istanbul. But we weren't prepared for what hit us when we touched down at the airport in Istanbul for the return match. It was chaos. There were Turkish fans everywhere and they were all shouting and waving their 'Welcome to Hell' banners. We got on the coach and they all chased us, they chased us for miles. I was more surprised by it all than scared; it was an experience.

The night before the game in we got death threats at the hotel. When the phone rang in the room, I just handed it to Incey and he gave whoever was calling an earful.

The atmosphere at thé Ali Sami Yen stadium was pretty wired, but Giggs was much more used to intimidation from opposing fans in the stands of their ground than at the arrival lounges of airports.

In the stadium there was an incredible atmosphere. In fact, I really loved it. A lot of the press said we were intimidated by the atmosphere. But it didn't worry me; the louder it is, the more I prefer it. It was brilliant there. Well, brilliant for them. The chants went all round the ground, everyone singing together like a choir, with all these drums going all the time.

If United weren't intimidated, however, they played like they were, and were unable to produce the sort of cohesive passing movements that had become their trademark. If fact, with 84 minutes

gone, Ferguson put Dion Dublin on for Roy Keane and United started trying to long-ball a goal. The match ended 0–0 and United were out of Europe. It didn't stop the intimidation from the Turkish fans.

They were a fanatical bunch all right, the Turks. On the ride back to the airport they threw all sorts of things at the coach. Brucey had his head against the window and someone threw a rock at him which cracked the window. God knows what would have happened if we'd turned them over.

The whole thing was a terrible cock-up. After beating us they went into the Champions' League and only scored one goal in six matches, which showed they weren't up to much.

Galatasaray had worked a fine game plan against United, but Premiership clubs couldn't get hold of the blueprint. United won 13 of their first 15 matches and for a while it looked unthinkable that anyone could catch them.

But we had to be careful. The press had built us up so much – saying that by Christmas we'd won it, we were the greatest, the best team ever – so there had to be a backlash. And it came. The press just started to stir things up. Eric got sent off, we lost the Coca-Cola Cup, Andrei got sent off, we lost to Blackburn and suddenly we were a bunch of moaners who didn't deserve to win anything, let alone the Treble we were going for.

A lot of managers started saying that you never get anything from referees if you go to Old Trafford. But I don't think any team gets any favours. You have to go out and play to win, and fight

for every decision just like all great teams – like Liverpool did in the 1980s – and if that means being called moaners and whingers, then so be it. We had so many players in that team who were so determined that I think people took it the wrong way. In fact I think it was good for us, it brought us even closer together and made us more of a team.

From March onwards we didn't worry about getting a good press. It became like a state of siege; everyone hated us, and I think that gave us motivation. Not that we needed any. The thing about football at the level we play is that every single game is vital, and every game Manchester United plays in is a Cup Final. Every ground we go to is full and there's this jealousy that comes with Manchester United's success. We are the team to beat, and that gets us as pumped up as the other team. You get fired up, you're desperate to win, and you tend to express your disappointment if things go against you. So it's not that we moan, it's just the emotions of the game.

United's answer to the critics was on the pitch. As well as dominating the League, Giggs and co were putting together a solid Cup run, reaching the semi final of the FA Cup having only conceded one goal. Oldham were their opponents in the Wembley semi and the Lancashire club looked that they'd got the measure of their more illustrious opponents, leading the match 1–0 with a minute of extra time to run.

**Mark Hughes came from nowhere and nearly burst the back of net. That's the thing about United, then and now: several of us can be having a horrible game but someone will do something brilliant to save us. And from the replay which we won 4–1 we just seemed to get stronger and stronger.**

The League title race, however, wasn't as clear cut as it had been the season before. United only won three games in a nine-match spell that let their nearest rivals, Blackburn, start closing what had once looked like an insurmountable gap. What really made fans sit up and realise that there was a title race was United's loss at Wimbledon.

**We should have wrapped things up in the League earlier than we did by winning against Wimbledon. We went out against them knowing Blackburn had lost at Southampton and that if we won, that was more or less it. But it was a horrible pitch, a horrible game, and they stopped us from playing. It was frustrating all round and they won 1–0.**

**The derby against City and a tough match at Elland Road followed, and things looked far from being all over. Then Eric came back from suspension, scored against City, and against Leeds we gave perhaps our best performance of the season. They put Fairclough on Eric, but even though he didn't get that much room for himself they were so worried about him they gave room to Sparky and Andrei and I. That's another brilliant thing about United – no one really knows what to do against us. Shut down one person and another will do the business.**

A black spot for the Welshman was that, although he was a regular in the side and playing a major part in their success, by May he still hadn't scored a League goal. He changed that at Portman Road in United's third-to-last game.

**It may seem strange to say it about a toe-poke from five yards, but I was pretty chuffed with that goal. What pleased me most was that I was getting into goalscoring positions, the Lineker and Rush places where you can do damage. I remember it well because we'd not really done well at Ipswich in the past and when we went 1–0 behind it was always going to be tough. But then we got one back and I managed to score with about 15 minutes to go. Then the manager substituted me. I think I hadn't passed to someone or something. It's not nice being subbed, especially if you don't think you're having a bad game and I didn't react too well to being taken off, which isn't like me at all. I didn't get into too much trouble for it, mind. The manager knew that my reaction was because I wanted the same thing as him – another title for United.**

The title was nearly won for United, but Blackburn were still in with a whimper if they could beat Coventry on Sunday 3 May, in a televised match. If they lost it, however, the title was United's.

I watched the game round at a friend's house. I think there were about six or seven of us, just me and my mates. After we'd won I rang my mum up, and went down to the local pub for a few drinks and then everyone ended up at Steve Bruce's house again. And just like the year before we had a game the next day!

United paraded their second successive Premiership trophy in front of the Old Trafford crowd the following evening. Giggs' only gripe is that the match was played on a Monday. He was brought up on Saturday afternoon football, kick off at three o'clock, and that's the way he likes it.

There's little chance of the Cup Final ever being played on a Monday night, and at 3 pm on Saturday 14 May, United faced Chelsea for the chance to win the Double for the first time in their history. By now, 20-year-old Giggs seemed a veteran in the team, but this was a new experience.

What a day that was, my first FA Cup Final. From the Monday before, it was madness: interviews, TV appearances, pictures for people. There were so many photographers at the training ground, it was just this huge build-up all week. United had already been to Wembley three times that year, and I hadn't been happy with any of my contributions. I was desperate to prove to myself that I could play at Wembley. I'd been substituted in the Coca-Cola Cup Final earlier in the season when we'd lost to Aston Villa and in the Charity Shield, and I'd only really come into the FA semi in extra time. The manager had a quiet word before the game. He just said: 'Come on, let's get this Wembley jinx of yours out of the way. Just play your normal game.'

We weren't affected by the fact that we could do the Double that day. There were no nerves at all. That pressure all seemed to lift after we lost the chance of the treble in the Coca-Cola Cup Final. In the dressing room before, we were quite relaxed; it was like we knew we were going to win it. With United every game is a big game, so you get used to it, but this was special. You could see it in everyone's eyes. I'm quite quiet in the dressing room so I just sat there, thinking about the game. We were all pretty calm really, there was no-one sort of screaming and shouting.

In the first half Chelsea outplayed us, but in the second we changed things around a bit. After Eric scored the first penalty we knew there was still plenty of work to do, but after the second one I think we knew the Double was in the bag. Eric loves taking penalties, he loves the pressure, and when he steps up you just know the ball's going to end up in the back of the net. I've taken two myself for United, scored one and missed one. The one I missed was in the FA Cup against Southampton in 1992 in a penalty shoot-out. I hit the target but it only just got there, it wasn't very good at all. I was only 17 and I couldn't think about anything else for weeks. It was terrible.

Anyway, luckily it was Eric taking the penalties at Wembley and from then on we enjoyed ourselves. Really enjoyed ourselves. When the final whistle blew and we had won 4-0 and secured the Double, the feeling was brilliant. We jumped around, sprayed each other with water, put a silly wig on the Boss's head and when we followed Steve Bruce up the steps, it suddenly struck me how lucky I was to be there. After all, if things had gone slightly differently I might have been playing for City.

giggs and fergie

# chapter ten

**The Boss sometimes joins in a five-a-side during training. It's a nightmare if he's on your side. He's a cheat. He just stands by the goal and knocks the ball in. If we're picking teams, he's always picked last. But his teams usually win, for some reason.**

He's joking, of course. Giggs has nothing but respect for his manager. Ask him if Ferguson has any weaknesses and, without hesitation, he says no. None at all.

Giggs has been at the club almost as long as Ferguson. He has seen the Scotsman's influence at every level of the club, so is better qualified than most to appraise the manager's contribution to United's success.

**The Boss is different from any other Manchester United manager before him because he didn't come into the team thinking we need success and we need it straight away. He started developing the Youth team. He realised that we had scouts all over the British Isles, but that we hardly had any in Manchester. When he arrived at United, Manchester City had a better youth policy. Ferguson had a really good youth system at Aberdeen and he put a similar one into practice here straight away. He changed everything. I remember when I was still at school training twice a week. On a Tuesday night for example, he'd be there, watching the training at the gym and chatting to the players. He knew all of us by name when we were schoolboys. There were a lot of kids there, but he made each one feel wanted. It really fired us up. He put time and effort into it; Manchester United would be playing a game on the Saturday afternoon, and he'd be watching the A team or the B team on Saturday morning. I don't think any other manager would do that.**

**He'd have a go at me, as well. I would be 15 or 16 and playing against guys in the first team, and he might decide to really tear a strip off me in front of the others. I used to feel really low sometimes, but I realise now he was doing it to toughen me up. You need to be very mentally tough when you're a football player and he was seeing to that. He put me with lads who were physically bigger than me to see how I'd react. To see if I could handle both the physical and mental challenge. He does it to all the young players who come through to see if they're strong enough to make the grade.**

**He also protected me physically. When I was a schoolboy, he called me into his office and said that he had worked out I'd played 85 games that season and it was too many. I couldn't tell what he was on about at the time because I felt as if I could play double that number. But he had had an experience with a young player at Aberdeen who was brilliant as a kid but who got burnt out when too much of him was asked too soon. So when I broke into the first team, he was always careful to rest me, dropping me to sub or off the team completely when he thought I was getting a bit jaded. You see, if you're not feeling well or an injury is nagging at you, it's up to you to say something. But I never would because I always wanted to play. There have been times when I have got fed up when the Gaffer's said: 'I'm not going to play you this week.' There were other times, though, he told me not to play and he was absolutely right. I wasn't up to it and and he seems to be able to see straight through me and read that. He's always honest about it. He'll have a quiet word with you in advance to say he's going to drop you and why. During the week, he'll pull you into his office and say, 'Listen, I'm playing Jordi' or 'You need a break.'**

It wasn't only when Giggs was a youngster that he was dropped from the team or put on the subs' bench. It still happens occasionally. Giggs has always responded well to being left out – which is just what the manager wants.

If you haven't been playing well then you've got to accept it, really. But if you feel you've been doing pretty well and he drops you or puts you on the substitutes' bench, you think to yourself: 'Why is he dropping me?' If you go and see him, he'll explain. He's dropped me a couple of times, not when I've been playing badly but when I've been not playing particularly well. He does it to buck you up. The others are playing games and you're left in the stands or on the bench, and you think, 'I don't like this'. You start trying much harder so you can get back into the team, and carry on like that so it doesn't happen again. That's good management. Part of his job is to get the best out of you, and he does it very well.

He's the biggest influence on my career, without a doubt. It didn't matter that I was three or four years younger than the players I was playing against. He had great belief in me. He just told me to do what I was good at and not worry about how old, or how big, or how famous the others were. It really helped me to develop fast.

You can go to see him whenever you want, for whatever reason. His door is always open. When you sign for the club, he says: 'If you've got any problems – it doesn't matter if it's not football, if you've got any problems at home or in your social life – come and see me or any of the staff. It's our job.' And I have done that. I've gone in to see him if ever I've needed any advice about things. I can honestly say that he's become something of a father figure to me. Definitely.

The Boss is fantastic at motivating us before matches. He drives us on and stops us becoming complacent. He's always asking us if we feel hungry enough for the challenge ahead and tells us that if we don't, there are five people he knows who do. He'll give a half-hour team-talk an hour and a half before kick-off in the changing room. We'll all be sitting round and he's standing in front of us; he doesn't wave his arms round or anything, but he's got such charisma you just listen to him. He'll talk about tactics and where he expects us to be at corners. He will discuss the other team a little as well. If one of the players hasn't been playing well recently he'll talk about it, right there in front of everybody else. But he won't have a go at you, he'll encourage you. Then he'll start talking about where we are in the League, and where he expects us to be. And he'll say things like, 'These

are the best times of your life, so make the most of them.' And, 'You don't want to think with two minutes to go that you're tired because you're still young. You'll regret it if you don't give it everything.' Or, 'You're playing for the best club in the world, so play like you're playing for the best club in the world.' When we go out onto the pitch we're really fired up.

Half-time talks are a different story. The manager's usually very relaxed when we're 1–0 down at half time. It's very rare that we play badly, really, but if we're not playing so well and we're 1–0 down at half time, he'll say something like, 'We can go out in the second half and score three.' He's much angrier if we're 1–0 ahead and not playing well. He loses his temper – he shouts a lot. If you're not playing well, or you've not passed to someone who'd have scored, he'll tell you all about it. He usually chooses two or three players who aren't playing well and focuses on them. It works – it really gets us going.

He shouts at us when we lose. Man United aren't expected to lose. Sometimes he keeps us in 10 or 15 minutes, shouting at us. Other times, though, he'll just say 'I'll see you on Monday' and walk off. That's much worse because you'd rather get it over with. If he says that, it's hanging over you all weekend. You know you're in for a hard time when you get back to work.

Tactically, he's unbelievable. He can spot things going wrong so fast, plug gaps and see openings. If I'm getting no change out of a full back, he'll get me to swap wings or bring me inside. He communicates what's wrong to the players really effectively. At half time in the 1994 Cup Final, for example, the Boss said to me: 'You can win this game for us.' What he meant was not that he expected some amazing bit of skill from me, but that a simple alteration in my position could make all the difference. In the first half, Chelsea's midfield was running the game. Andrei and I were too far out on the wings, giving them too much space inside. So he moved us in. They didn't change tack and they didn't get a kick in the second half. He's also very good at spotting your individual weaknesses; something I've got to work on is my vision of what's going on around me.

When I first got into the team, it was just head down and take people on – which the crowd likes when it comes off, but which is pretty pointless when it doesn't. The Boss had a word with me and said, 'You don't have to beat a player every time. Sometimes make a simple pass and that will keep the defender guessing – he won't be certain of what you're trying to do.' It's something you learn with experience, knowing when to take someone on and when to pass it. And the Boss is very good at making sure you learn quickly. He's a brilliant teacher.

One problem that Ferguson faces at United is having an embarrassment of riches: a surplus of good players trying to get into the team. You might feel that there could be some resentment when he buys new players for the club who are a threat to existing players' places. Not a bit of it, if you believe Giggs.

The Boss has always drummed it into us that no player's place in the team is safe, so you have to play well to justify your selection, however highly you're rated. He's also brilliant in the transfer market – he always buys players who are versatile. If he buys someone you think is a threat to your position, you've just got to look at it as a challenge. If you're both playing well then there will be room for you both in the team, even if one of you has to move out of your normal role. It just serves to fire you up, because everybody wants to play for Manchester United.

Giggs is one of the few established players in the Premiership to have played his entire career (which now goes back over 10 years) at one club under one manager. He's hardly going to criticise the guy, but you can tell from the way he speaks that experience has left him with a profound respect for the man, as well as deep gratitude for all the help Ferguson has given him.

From the moment he came to my house that day when I was 14, he has helped me develop into the player I am and I know that he will continue to help me. There's no doubt about it: without him I wouldn't be where I am today.

# season four 1994/95

# chapter eleven

When United started the 1993/94 season, it wasn't so much a case of "can they win the League again this year?" from press and pundits. It was more "who can possibly stop them?" It was a similar deal with Giggs, who had become something of a national institution, famous even with non-football fans for his blend of good looks and talented feet. "The frightening thing," everyone was saying, "is that he can only get better." Unfortunately it wasn't to be.

**The 1994/95 season was a nightmare, not just for the club but for me personally. We were runners up in the League and runners up in the FA Cup, and I guess for a lot of teams that would have been the best ever season in their history. But for us, after winning the Double the year before, it was a devastating blow.**

**For me personally it was a complete disaster too, because for the first time in my career I suffered from injury problems. My original injury came in a match against Ipswich right at the start of the season when I got a calf strain. Up to that point in my career I'd been almost injury free, but after that I just got one injury after another. I developed problems with my ankle, Achilles tendon and hamstring – all on the same leg – which meant that I was not only missing matches but also training sessions, which makes it all the more difficult to keep fully fit.**

After so much domestic success for United, again the public was expecting great things of them in the European Cup – especially as this year they didn't have to enter the qualifying stages but went straight into the round robin Champions' League group with Gothenberg, Galatasaray (again) and Spanish giants Barcelona.

Giggs made a good start to the Champions' League campaign by scoring two goals in the 4–2 first-match win over Gothenberg at Old Trafford. United looked good in attack, but conceding two goals at home hinted that defensive frailties might prove their undoing. Giggs was again in the side for United's return to Galatasary, which ended in the same result as the year before – but this time the 0–0 scoreline was a positive reward for Ferguson's men. Next up was Barcelona – a match which Giggs missed through injury.

We played well against Barcelona at home, and we were unlucky to get a draw rather than a win. If we'd won that game I think we'd have got through to the quarter finals, no problem. The result meant we needed at least a draw in Barcelona two weeks later to keep on course for a place in the next round. But it wasn't to be.

For that game we were missing quite a few players. I hadn't played for two weeks and I hadn't trained either, but I was desperate to play. I'd missed the Barcelona game at Old Trafford and I didn't want to miss this one, so I told the manager I was fit, that I was OK, even though in truth I wasn't. In fact I was probably only 50% fit and it turned out to be a terrible game. In that sort of situation it's not that you're pretending to be fit, it's more that you want to be involved so badly that you convince yourself you're OK. Sometimes you'll think you're taking a risk with an

injury but 10 minutes into the game you'll realise that you'll be OK, that you're fit again. Other matches, you'll come back and two minutes into the game you'll realise it's not right. This was one of those games. I got substituted in the end, and I deserved to be.

It wasn't the best stage in the world to die on. The atmosphere in the Nou Camp was incredible; there were 120,000 people there and I'd never played in front of so many. But we were beaten by four goals, and it turned out to be a nightmare, a night to forget. The trip back on the plane was really difficult, we were all really down.

A 3–1 loss in Gothenberg sealed United's fate, and their 4–0 revenge over Galatasaray proved hollow as it wasn't enough to save them from another early exit from the competition. Giggs puts the blame partially on UEFA's limit on foreign players, partly on United's injury problems, and partly simply on poor quality performances throughout the team.

It was my first ever experience of the Champions' League and it was a really frustrating campaign, because for every game we had two or three players out. At this level of football you need your full side and we never had that. We didn't have Eric, I was injured for a lot of the matches and then there was the three foreigners rule which meant we couldn't play the team who had actually won the League. I mean it was ridiculous. I've lived in England most of my life, but I was classed as an "assimilated foreigner" because I'd been in the country more than 10 years. We ended up having to leave important players out of vital matches, players of the quality of Peter Schmeichel, Mark Hughes and Andrei Kanchelskis. They've changed the rule now, so hopefully we'll do a bit better in the future.

It wasn't the only frustration: I had injury problems from start to finish of that season. It wasn't as if I had one bad injury I had to recover from, and I'm grateful for that. But all season I just had these annoying little niggly injuries. I'd often have a late fitness test on the Friday before the game and end up playing. In the end I played 31 games, but I was never fully fit and my game suffered because I wanted to play so much. When you're a young you just want to play games, and you think you're fit when you're not. I guess I've learnt to be a bit more patient now.

Two incidents that season really shocked the footballing world. The first was the signing of striker Andy Cole from United's Championship rivals Newcastle.

The whole club got a lift when we signed Andy completely out of the blue. Halfway through the season it was suddenly announced and we were all staggered – in fact, I think the whole of football was stunned. We couldn't believe it. He was doing so well for Kevin Keegan. I wasn't surprised the Boss bought him, I was more surprised that his manager let him go. I remember we were

playing an away game in the FA Cup against Sheffield United and after the match one of their players told us he'd heard some rumours about Andy signing for us. Then the next day it was in the papers. Just like that.

It was hard for Andy. He didn't do for us what he was doing for Newcastle, but he he hasn't played badly. He was in the side that won the 1995/96 Double, after all. The thing is that when he arrived at the club everyone expected him to score 35 goals a season, but it never happened because we don't play the same way as Newcastle. It was hard for him because we're not a club that has one player scoring all the goals. There are five or six players who get them, because of the way we play. We move around and swap positions, and play as a team. Alan Shearer wouldn't score 35 goals a season for United.

The furore had just died down when a new football story hit the front as well as the back pages of the newspapers. Eric Cantona, having been sent off at Selhurst Park during a match against Crystal Palce, suddenly leapt into the crowd feet first in a retaliatory attack on a Palace fan. Giggs was playing in South London that day.

To be honest, I was right over on the other side of the pitch when it happened because I was playing right wing that night, so I didn't see the incident that clearly. I heard the crowd shouting after Eric had been sent off and when I turned round there was a big bunch of

players over by the touchline. I didn't know what was going on. The first time I saw what had really happened was on the television the next day. A few of the players had told me what he'd done, but I couldn't believe it when I saw it. It was very surprising what Eric did. Afterwards he was very quiet in the dressing room, but then again so were we all. We desperately needed to win, we'd gone 1–0 up and we'd let them get back to 1–1. So that was enough to depress us anyway. When Matthew Simmonds, the guy that Eric kicked, was eventually prosecuted himself he attacked the prosecuting barrister. That showed him to be a thug – but I think everybody knew that anyway.

It definitely had an effect on the outcome of the Championship that year. We were chasing Blackburn all the way but, although we kept up the pressure, we really missed Eric. I'm certain that if he hadn't been banned we'd have won the title. I was injured again at the end of the season and I remember missing the last few matches.

United certainly needed Giggs in those matches as the title race went right to the wire. United had to win at West Ham and hope that Blackburn failed to beat Liverpool to lift a third successive title. Blackburn duly lost 2–1 to Liverpool... but West Ham, thanks to some marvellous saves by Ludek Miklosko and some poor United finishing, failed to beat the Hammers and the final score was 1–1. Giggs didn't travel to London that day because he couldn't bear to.

I was sat at home watching the game on the last day of the season with my friends. We had so many chances but we just couldn't put them away. It was terrible, especially with Blackburn losing to Liverpool. It was an empty feeling because the whole season was lost just on one day. You look back on the season and you wonder if you could have done anything different. Because one more goal in any number of games would have made the difference. I went into a bit of a sulk. My mates were telling me not to worry, just get fit for the FA Cup Final. It was some consolation, but not much.

United's failure in the League destroyed their hopes of a double Double, but having beaten Crystal Palace in a contentious semi final, they still had the FA Cup Final to look forward to. Giggs was desperate to play but still had to shake off his umpteenth injury of the season.

I had a week to get fit, but the manager only had a week to lift the whole team. Everyone was so down. I think if we'd won the League we would have won the Final the following week against Everton. But when your season goes down the drain and then you have to pick everything up for one more game, it's hard. It was only six days later and Everton were really fired up for the game.

During training on the Thursday before the Final, my hamstring went again. I went to the manager and said to him: 'Listen, there's no way I'm going to be fit, so you might as well let someone else play.' So he said, 'I'll put you on the bench, and maybe we'll give you 20 minutes or so.' It was difficult to say that to him because of course I wanted to play, but I'd learnt my lesson. In the end, I came off the bench at half time and played quite well, but I couldn't turn it round and we lost 1–0.

It was disappointing, especially walking up the steps and getting a losers' medal instead of a winners' one. At the end of the day, the manager just said goodbye to us in the changing room, and said have a good night, have a good holiday. That's the last I saw of him until pre-season training. We all felt so terrible we just wanted to get off home. But when you feel like that, when you don't get any reward from a long, tough season in which you've worked very hard, you learn from it. It made me determined never to have an experience like that one again. And I know it had the same effect on a lot of the other players, too. Losing is difficult when you're a winner.

# a day in the life

## chapter twelve

On an ordinary weekday, that's to say a non-match day, I wake up at about nine o'clock. I have an alarm clock which I set for just after nine but I usually wake up just before it goes off. I've got a good body clock. I'm not the sort of person who jumps out of bed: I'll sit up and watch television for 10 or 15 minutes. I usually watch GMTV, unless there's something special on like the Olympics.

Then I go downstairs and make some breakfast. It's no big deal. I usually just have cereals. We're not told what to have for breakfast, but I wouldn't fancy a fry-up at that time in the morning anyway. When we get to the training ground, there's tea and toast prepared for us and cereals as well, so I don't go too big on breakfasts at home.

Next I have a wash, clean my teeth and get ready to go out. It doesn't take me long to get ready – about two minutes or so. I just have to throw on a track suit, really, because I'm only going to the training ground. It takes me 10 minutes to drive to our training ground at the Cliff. I'm thankful it's pretty near my house – I don't like to waste too much time travelling.

I'm not that good in the morning. It usually takes me quite a time to wake up. Some days when I arrive at training just before 10 o'clock, I haven't completely woken up. But I really enjoy training. In fact I love it – I certainly don't wake up in the morning thinking 'oh no'. I'm usually very positive about the day ahead.

When I get into the changing room I'll sit down, make myself a cup of tea, get changed and chat to the other players. Just general chit-chat: what's on television; what's in the newspapers. We always take the mickey out of each other a bit, too, especially when there's a story about one of us in the press.

We start training at about 10.30. First we warm up for about 15 minutes. This comprises of jogging, stretching and a few runs. It's important to warm up a bit and stretch before you start training, because otherwise it's easy to pull a muscle – especially in the winter. Nobody wants to miss any matches from making such a stupid mistake so we're all pretty good at going through the routines.

Brian Kidd is brilliant at leading training. He studies all sorts of methods and has all sorts of ideas. I feel frustrated if I haven't come away from a session having learnt something or improved an aspect of my game. After warming up, we play a bit of possession, a game with two teams playing on a little pitch with no goals and just trying to keep hold of the ball. It's really good practice for playing the United way as it involves not giving the ball away too much to the opposition.

After that, we'll usually play five-a-side. We really take it seriously, because we split into the young lads and the old lads and there's always a bit of competition for places in the side. I'm still in with the young lads – I'm just about holding in there. Our team usually wins, though the older guys often try to cheat. They're always claiming it's their ball when it goes off. Sometimes it gets quite rough, but Kiddo will call it a day before there's any serious violence!

Then maybe we'll do some running – short running, not long stuff – and a bit of shooting afterwards. Some of the lads go in at this point, but most of us stay out. It's good practice. You can always improve your shooting, especially on your wrong foot, and it's useful for the keepers. Sometimes there's some specialist training with Kiddo afterwards. A lot of the time a few of us will stay back – Jordi, David

117

Beckham, Philip Neville and me maybe – and do a bit of practise on our crossing.

Towards the end of the season, when we're playing two or even three games a week, training becomes much slower: no more than a quick jog, some five-a-side and then lying on the treatment table. At that stage, you really can't work on your technique – which everyone needs to do, no matter what level they've reached. All of the players keep saying we play too much football and that being too tired to train properly is not good for the game. But nobody seems to listen.

We finish training about noon. Some of the lads will have dinner upstairs, some will go straight home. I usually go up and have dinner, till about just after one.

When you leave the building there's usually quite a few fans in the car park, shouting your name and asking you to sign autographs. There are hundreds some days. You can't sign them every day, but you try to do it most of the time. Sometimes you might have to rush off. Most days at least six or seven players will do it. You have to try to get round to everyone there – you just start at one end and go down the line until you've finished. It's not annoying. I'm in no big hurry most of the time, so I'm quite happy to do it.

Then I drive home again. Sometimes I'll just watch television in the afternoon. I like flicking between MTV and Sky Sports. Other times I'll go round a mate's house and we'll sit and chat or watch TV. I might go out shopping if I fancy buying some clothes.

I usually go round to a friend's house for dinner – my friend Dave's mum often cooks for me. She does a good rice, does Dave's mum, Chinese style. Or steak and chips. The club doesn't try to control what I eat. A lot of the older players are a bit bigger and they have to watch their weight and be a bit careful; they can't go out and eat fatty foods all the time. But I've got very low body fat, so there's not too much to worry about. The club reckons you should be below 15 per cent and I'm only eight per cent, so I'm OK. In the two to three days running up to a match, we're told to eat a lot of pasta, grilled chicken, fish and a fair amount of fruit, which is fortunate for me because I like that sort of food.

The rule at Manchester United is that you can't go out for three nights before a game. I mean out out, drinking and that. There's no iron fist treatment – no one checks on you or anything. I don't think many of the players actually do break the rules. This restriction can be a pain though, particularly since we play so many games on a Sunday and my mates are all out on Friday and Saturday night. Actually, they're pretty good to me. They don't tempt me out.

On a weekday night, some of my mates usually come round and we just mess around together. We play pool – I've got my own table, which is nice. We watch a bit of TV or catch a video. I usually go to bed at 11, or half past, and go to sleep around 12. I get to sleep pretty easily – I don't suffer from insomnia. There's a dietician at the club who tells you what to eat and what not to eat and he recommends eight to 10 hours' sleep a night. I usually sleep for nine – which fits in quite nicely. I actually feel it on the pitch if I haven't had enough sleep in the week, so I suppose it's an important part of our training.

If there's a match, the day is rather different. I usually wake up between half nine and 10 o'clock. I'll sit in bed and watch whatever's on television. I'm not really thinking about the game at that point. I'm quite relaxed. I get up at about quarter to 11, have a shower and then put on a suit. I leave for the ground at about 11.35 – it takes me about 20 minutes to get there.

If you are carrying a slight knock, you are taken for a late fitness test at the Cliff earlier in the morning. You usually know how you feel and whether you're up for it, but our physiotherapist generally has something to say. One of the worst injuries of my career was the one I got against Manchester City in 1993. I had the ball on the wing, cut inside and shot. Steve McMahon came across to block me, put his foot up to stop the ball and, with my follow-through, I kicked the studs on the bottom of his boot. It made contact with the top of my foot, which has very little protection, and I think I pulled a ligament. Ask any footballer and they'll say if that was your worst injury, you've been incredibly lucky.

I only have to look around the Cliff to see how lucky I am. David Johnson and Ben Thornley, two of our best young players, have both had cruciate ligament damage. Johnno had to sit round for six months. The longest I've been out is two weeks. Even then I got frustrated watching the lads going out and training, so God knows how I'd feel if I was out as long as Johnno.

If I'm not injured and it's a home game, I'll meet up with the players and the staff at Old Trafford and we'll have lunch together in the Grill Room. It's very informal. We just watch TV and chat to each other while we're eating. That takes 25 minutes to half an hour. Then I'll go down to the players' lounge where all the papers are laid out, and there's another television. I'll read the papers, and watch TV – Football Focus maybe – for about an hour, and have a chat with the other players. We like to have a bit of a laugh at this stage, to unwind a bit. Some of the players also like to put a bet on the horses. It's probably the worst part of the day for me. I just can't wait to get out on to the pitch and get on with it.

At about half past one, Brian Kidd calls us into the changing room. For 25 minutes the manager does his team talk. He'll name the team, tell you a bit about the opposition and talk about things like set pieces. Then he'll go off and you won't see him

for 45 minutes or so. I've never worked out where he goes – maybe it's into his office or something.

Then we'll sit in the changing room until we go out for a warm-up at about half past two. Each player has got his own warm-up routine and there's a gym in the changing rooms where you can mess around with the ball and do some stretches. Then about 20 minutes before kick-off, we go out on the pitch to kick the ball about and get a feel of the pitch. You can see the crowd building up and feel the atmosphere getting hotter. Then you go back to the changing room and get into your kit.

I never get nervous before matches – or at least, I rarely do. The first game I played, when I was substitute, I really felt the butterflies. Then, after hundreds of games without feeling a thing, I felt really jittery at the end of the 1995/96 season when we had to beat Middlesbrough and Liverpool to win the Double. It's curious, I don't know why I felt nervous again. Maybe it was something to do with getting so close to it the year before and coming out with nothing.

Next comes the bit that you'll know all about. We play football for 90 minutes with a 15 minute break in between. That's the best part of the day, usually. When we finish the match the manager will talk to us for 15 minutes or so. If we've won, which is usually the case, he'll congratulate us. If we lose, he'll shout at us – or he'll just say 'see you on Monday' and he'll be off.

Then you have a shower, get changed and go into the players' lounge to see your family and friends. You get a few lounge tickets to give out for matches. You spend about half an hour, maybe 45 minutes together, have a drink and a bit of a chat. Some of the players go off for a meal together, but I just go home with my mates.

Ideally, after that, I just go to the local pub to have a few drinks and wind down. I'll usually get something to eat there and at closing time I just go home. I'm usually ready for bed by that time.

# season five 1995/96

# chapter thirteen

Most of the neutral fans and the press loved it when United failed to win anything in 1994/95. During the close season, lots of people were talking about the end of the Ferguson era when the manager sold three of their best players, Paul Ince, Mark Hughes and Andrei Kanchelskis, without calling up a single replacement.

**It felt different turning up for pre-season training without Incey, Sparkie and Andrei, but I wasn't worried. It was difficult because they were all good friends, especially Incey who I roomed with, but losing team-mates is part and parcel of football. Since I've been in the team a lot of great players have moved on, and of course you miss them at first but you move on quickly. The papers loved it but we just carried on as normal. There were plenty of youngsters waiting in the wings to take their places.**

**One story the press particularly got its teeth into that summer was the phone poll in the Manchester Evening News which claimed 55 per cent of United fans wanted Ferguson sacked. What a load of rubbish that was. For a start, the majority of those phone calls were probably from City fans. I think we all knew the poll was a complete joke and we didn't take any notice of it at all, unlike the national papers who all picked up on it.**

United's detractors were even more pleased when Ferguson's team failed to impress in their opening fixture, losing 3–1 at Aston Villa. Giggs wasn't there that day.

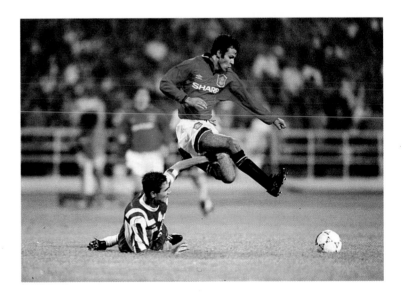

I was still injured and didn't play and the lads lost 3–1. Straight away everyone was writing us off, including Alan Hansen, who made his 'Kids don't win titles' comment on Match of the Day. But people just looked at the result. It may have been 3–1, but we had a lot of chances that day with a very young side. I mean the first time we won the League we were bottom after three games. It's a long season and we knew that, but I didn't play in that game, Andy Cole didn't play, Eric Cantona and Steve Bruce didn't play. Key players. And we knew once we had a full team we'd be a different proposition. I suppose in a way Alan Hansen was right to say what he said. If you look back at football history, young teams usually don't win things, but we knew just how good our kids were and obviously he didn't.

Then we lost 3–0 to Second Division York City at Old Trafford in the Coca-Cola Cup. I wasn't playing again, and we put out a very, very young side. Frankly we thought it would be a really easy game, but York played superbly and they deserved to win. It was humiliating, but that's cup football and on the night it was their night. With a stronger team we'd have beaten them without a doubt.

The Coca-Cola Cup was one thing; it was the second season Ferguson had put out young players in the competition and he admitted it wasn't exactly his top priority. The UEFA Cup was a different matter. Ferguson was desperate to make United's name more feared on the continent after two years of humiliation.

When we played Rotor Volgograd away it was my first game back, and I missed a lot of chances. We played well and were confident, and were pretty pleased to come away 0–0, even though we'd have liked the away goal. But in the second leg we had a few players missing and we just didn't perform on the night. They went 2–0 up and you just can't let that happen in Europe, so we probably deserved what we got.

What we got was a 2-2 draw. The only consolation was that our proud unbeaten-at-home-in-Europe run was still going, thanks to a late goal by Peter Schmeichel. I was on the edge of the box when he scored. He's done it before in training so I wasn't too surprised, but he really panicked their defence. For the whole of the second half we'd been pumping crosses in, we'd hit the bar and they'd crossed two off the line... so we just needed to try something a bit different. Having Peter Schmeichel up for a corner certainly achieves that.

In between those two UEFA Cup matches I scored my first goal in the League for more than a year, which just shows what a rough time I'd had of it with injuries. I got the winner when we played Everton away and beat them 3–2, and it was a great feeling.

With the Reds out of two Cup competitions and Newcastle United setting the pace in the League, things weren't looking too good; but there was one thing to look forward to. The return of the magnificent seven, Eric Cantona, from suspension came on 1 October in the match against Liverpool at Old Trafford.

**It was a massive boost when Eric came back. The thing is that in this team, everything involving attacking goes through Eric. He's such a good player that the team revolves around him, so of course we were bound to miss him. He can score goals, he can make goals. He's such an intelligent player, so consistent. He makes all the difference. And he always seems to score the crucial goals; he has that skill that all great goalscorers have of being in the right place at the right time.**

**At around that time, the young players were starting to come in a lot and they did so well. I had played with them all in the Youth team and in the Reserves, and suddenly after those three players were sold they got their big chance. Instead of the manager having to buy players, he knew he had kids who were as good as anyone in the League. I think the Boss found a good mix of youth and experience. In one game I think there were seven players who were under 21 and that's exciting for a club. I don't think anyone at United was surprised at how well the young players did when they first came into the side; the surprise was at the consistency they showed all season.**

**I think it helped them that there were five or six of them coming into the team at the same time. On away trips at a club like Manchester United it can be quite daunting, but they all came in together so it wasn't like that. It was funny because they'd come up to me – because I'd recently been through it myself – and ask me things like what they should take on away trips. They used to ask me stuff like whether they should wear a club blazer or a tracksuit, that sort of thing.**

Newcastle had built up a huge lead in the table – at one point they were 12 points clear. But in the late winter and early spring, United started clawing their way back into the reckoning with a string of wins, many of them thanks to deciding goals by Cantona.

**I think the crucial match of the whole season was when we played Newcastle at St James' Park. In the build-up to that game, everyone was saying: 'Well, if you don't win that, it's all over.' I think we felt that way too. We knew we couldn't lose and that even if we got a draw we'd only have an**

outside chance. Everyone was saying what a daunting task, to go to St James' Park where they've won every game all season. But a team like Manchester United can go anywhere and win and we were confident that that's exactly what we were going to do.

In the first half we didn't even get out of our half. Peter Schmeichel was brilliant, he made so many vital saves, but it's no good having all that possession and all those shots if you don't score. We had our chance and Eric took it. That 1–0 win made it possible for us to win the title.

The atmosphere at St James' Park that night was great. There was so much tension and the Newcastle fans were tremendous. But I didn't feel sorry for them afterwards; you can't ever feel sympathy for your opponents. In our changing room after the game it was like we'd won a Cup Final. Everyone was congratulating each other and I remember that I just couldn't wait for the next game. For the last few months I had really felt that I was playing well again, and the nightmare of the season before was behind me.

There was only one major hiccough on the way to the title: a defeat at Southampton during which United changed their grey shirts for white and blue ones at half time, having just conceded a third goal with no reply. Giggs managed a goal back in the second half, but United ended up losing 3–1.

A lot was made of the grey kit and the fact that we changed at half-time, but the truth is that we simply didn't play well that day. Southampton were fighting for their lives and it's always hard to go to grounds like that. I don't think it would have made any difference if we'd been wearing the blue kit from the start, although it is true that it was difficult to pick each other out in the grey. I didn't like playing in it but that's no excuse. That's the thing about the Premiership, it doesn't matter who you play, bottom is capable of beating top. There are no easy games.

When Newcastle won the next day, the Championship race was neck-and-neck again. Every run-in is tense and this was no different. You become obsessed by it, it's with you wherever you go, whatever you do. But you've got to try and enjoy it as well, enjoy the challenge. If you don't enjoy it your football will suffer, you'll be too nervous. And believe me, we were enjoying it.

Our penultimate game was against Nottingham Forest at Old Trafford. We won 5–0, which meant

**Newcastle couldn't beat our goal difference. I got one of the goals, although I didn't really mean to. I saw Scholsey in the box and I just drilled it in. Scholsey didn't get to it but I think Mark Crossley thought he would, so when they both missed it just slipped in the corner. It was more satisfying than a 30-yard stonker in some ways because it was such a surprise... they all count anyway. The lads took the mickey but I told them I'd meant to place it right in the corner.**

It wasn't Giggs' last goal of the season. United faced Middlesbrough in the last game needing to avoid defeat to win the Championship. A second goal just after half-time virtually sealed the game, then in the 80th minute Giggs put paid to the most optimistic Geordie's hopes.

**It's probably my favourite goal ever because it was such a big occasion. I had a long run and then a shot from outside the box, and when it went in I felt 10 foot tall. It was so tense and I was so nervous before the match that it was a real relief when the season was finally over and we'd won it.**

**The United fans there that day made a difference. I think I've got a great relationship with the fans. From the first time I came into the team, they've always encouraged me, they've always been good to me. If you're having a bad patch and you do something special and they get behind you, it can change your whole game. It's strange having a relationship with 50,000 people, but you do feel close to them. Everywhere we go there are always thousands of them, and at home it's always a full house. Sometimes you just feel like you can't get beat, and if you do lose you're really conscious that you've let the fans down.**

Of course there were plenty of United fans at the FA Cup Final, which United reached by beating Glenn Hoddle's Chelsea in the semi final after going a goal behind. For Giggs, Wembley wasn't such a new experience anymore as he prepared to face Liverpool in one of the most keenly anticipated games for years.

**It was my third Final in a row, so I guess I am starting to get used to them, but the atmosphere and the occasion still make the hairs on the back of your neck stand on end. I remember being introduced to all the dignitaries and so**

on but they didn't say much to me, they just shook my hand and moved on. The Duchess of Kent asked me if I was looking forward to the game, but I can't remember what I said. You have a chat with them, but you're just thinking about the game. You just want to get started.

Like many games that are over-hyped, the game itself was a bit of a let-down. United may have won with a brilliant late volley from Cantona, but it was the only moment of the match that will live in the memory. United were criticised in some of the papers after the game.

**To be honest, I wasn't up early enough to see the papers. We realised that we'd played Liverpool twice and they'd outplayed us twice. So we had to stop them playing. They also did that to us a bit as well, mind you. We both cancelled each other out and it was always going to be decided by the odd goal. Luckily we got it, and once again it was Eric who kept cool.**

Giggs has so many medals stuffed away in a cupboard at his mum's house, you'd think he'd be sick of winning them. But he's finding silverware rather addictive.

**As always, it was a great feeling winning the Cup, you never tire of that. To win the second Double was incredible. Like the manager says, if you win, it just makes you want to go out and win more.**

# chapter fourteen

Ryan Giggs is still a very young man. Born in November 1973, he's 22 years old as we write this book: he'll probably have just turned 23 by the time the book is published. It's sometimes very difficult to remember how young he is, as he made his debut so long ago – back in 1991. Since then, Giggs has had an incredibly successful career. He now has three League titles, two FA Cups and a League Cup under his belt, a tally even top players usually can't match in a whole career. He's already won more trophies than Stanley Matthews, George Best and Gary Lineker ever did and he's only just started. The final tally could be phenomenal: Giggs stands to win more honours than any player ever before him.

What Giggs hasn't achieved yet is success on the European and international stage and he's yearning to make amends.

**The European Cup is our priority now. I desperately want to win it and everyone at the club feels the same. This doesn't mean that we can forget about the Premiership, because if we don't win the Champions' League we'll want to have a chance to have another crack at it the following season. But the European Cup is the one that we really want to go for.**

**We've been very disappointing in previous European campaigns, and we're very aware of it. But that just makes us all the more determined to do well in the future. We've taken on board the sort of mistakes we've made in the past and we don't want to repeat them. European football is very different from English football, and it's a question of adapting our game. We've got to learn to be more patient when playing foreign teams.**

**You might think it would be easy for us to lose interest in the League with all these Champions' League matches coming up, but that's not the case. The Boss is a great motivator, and it's his job to get us as fired up against Southampton as against Juventus. Not that he needs to really. With the squad we've got at United, you know that if you don't try your hardest in a League game the manager will always have someone who's trying harder in the squad – and he'll replace you. You don't want to miss a big European match because you didn't try hard enough in a Premiership one. So you tend to be fired up for every game. Every match is a Cup Final for Man United.**

Wales are hardly the Manchester United of League football; as we go to press they lie 70th in the FIFA World Rankings. Nevertheless, Giggs is hoping that he can win some international honours for his country in the future – or at least help them qualify for the Finals of a major tournament.

**I think we can qualify this time. Wales haven't been in the Finals for a long time, although they just missed out on a number of occasions. It's about time we did – and I mean to do my best to help us get to France. We've got Holland, Belgium, San Marino and Turkey in our group. We've got to play well at home and make sure we win all our games at Cardiff Arms Park, and then try to get a few results away. We've beaten Belgium**

before, and Holland aren't as good as they used to be, so I think we've got every chance.

On the domestic front, Manchester United look set to sweep much of the board for years to come. Giggs is certainly hopeful for the future.

**I don't see why we can't go from strength to strength and just carry on winning. We've got a great side, we've got a good mixture of youth and experience and the Boss has a keen eye for a good buy on the transfer market to keep everyone on their toes.**

**I think we've got to see Newcastle as the team to beat. Over the last few years they've got stronger every season. They've got great players there and wonderful support. Kevin Keegan's a fine manager – and having Alan Shearer in the side is bound to make a difference. Liverpool will be another team to look out for. They're a similar team to us in that they've got a good mixture of young and old players. They've got stronger over the last few seasons, too. Those two will be our main competitors, although there has been such a rash of signings recently that you don't know how the other teams will perform. There are so many unknown quantities in the League; maybe another team will come good and start pushing for the title.**

Whenever a player in the English League starts shining, there is speculation about him going abroad. Giggs is quick to stifle any such rumours about himself, and you can see that he means what he says.

**I never really think of leaving Manchester United. There are so many good players, we're winning so many trophies and the place is so well run. I can't see any point in even thinking about it. I love the club, I love the city and I'm very happy with the way things are going. It was my dream to play for Manchester United and I'm still enjoying every minute of it. Anyway, I don't think I've finished learning my trade; I've got a lot to learn. The manager is always pointing things out that I should or should not be doing.**

**The most important qualities in a professional footballer are determination and dedication. I had to work really hard at my football and I still do. Of course, skill is something you are born with, but you have to keep on practising if you really want to make the most of it.**

135

One man who desperately wants to see Giggs stay put is Alex Ferguson, but he's not losing much sleep about the Welshman leaving United. "He might need to sit down and ask himself a few pertinent questions," muses the United manager. "Like, would it be worth going to Italy and being subjected to the daily harassment and aggro that plagued Paul Gascoigne? Could he achieve anything more over there than he would at United? Would foreign football bring out the best in him and be a true test of his character and ability? Would he benefit from the experience, apart from in financial terms?

"There aren't many stadiums in the world, for instance, that can equal the splendour of Old Trafford," continues the manager. "I agree there are great sporting arenas in Spain and Italy, but I don't think any compare with the sense of theatre you are guaranteed at our place. It's hard to match. Certainly it would have to be one of Italy's top three clubs that could present Giggs with anything that comes close to it. Part of the foreign equation is that not very many British players find the continental game comfortable and often are unable to adjust. Only recently there have been classic examples in Ian Rush and Des Walker. Beyond doubt, this is proof for Ryan if he needs it that on the continent it is not all about mega money and living on Easy Street.

"After all, what are his aims?" concludes Ferguson. "They must include winning trophies, and he can do that here with United. Another understandable aim is to end his playing career wealthy and without a worry for the rest of his life. I believe we can achieve that for him, too. He's well down that particular road even now. So what else can Ryan want? There's maybe a curiosity about sampling what foreign soccer is all about. But really that's something to be considered when he is in his mid-twenties. When the stardust has gone and he can make a mature and proper decision for himself."

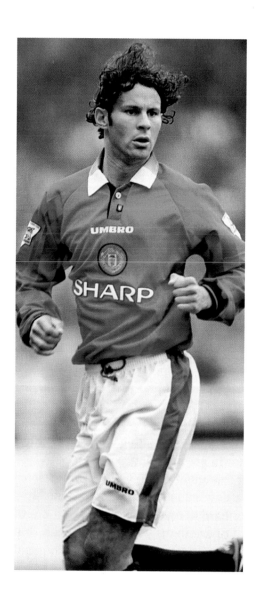

A couple of years ago, Italy undoubtedly boasted the strongest League in the world. It was also the most lucrative market for a player and acted as a magnet for some of the world's best. Now, however, with the cash injections from Sky and the resulting boom in the English game, the balance has shifted England's way, and that has had the effect of strengthening Giggs' resolve to remain in the North West.

**I watch Italian football sometimes and I like it, although I must say I'd rather watch a Premiership game. But I have no ambitions to go out there and play at the moment – especially as England is the place to be nowadays. You've only got to look at all the stars who are coming over here from abroad. A couple of years ago it would have been unthinkable that the likes**

of Vialli, Ravanelli and Di Matteo would be playing over here. It's got to be the best League in the world at the moment.

There's been a lot of debate about the number of foreigners in a team and whether this prevents home-grown youngsters from playing. But there's another side to the question; these foreigners can teach our youngsters a lot and improve the standard of British play. If you ask any of the apprentices at our club who's their favourite player, it's always Eric Cantona. If you ask them if they've learnt anything from him, they'll say, 'yeah, loads'. I've certainly learnt an enormous amount from him. People are saying that players from abroad stop youngsters from coming through, but as the kids have proved at Manchester United, if you're good enough, you'll play. If you're 18 and English and you're playing well you'll take the place of a 25-year-old Italian who isn't.

There's a football saying about taking each game as it comes and, no matter how many times it has been said before, you have to carry that philosophy with you, because a life in football can go horribly wrong at any time. While things are going your way, I believe you should enjoy them. Being a footballer is the best possible life. You get paid very well for doing what you love; you get time to yourself; you get to meet famous and interesting people and, if you play for Manchester United, you get to play alongside the best in the business.

Ask him about the long-term future, and naturally he's very unsure. The question bugs him a little, actually. There's every possibility that he won't have to hang up his boots for another 15 years, after all. Re-phrase the question, ask him what he hopes he will be doing, and he's much happier.

If you asked me 15 years ago if I'd be playing for Manchester United in 15 years time I could only have said I hope so. It's incredibly hard to say what I'll be doing when I'm 40, but I can tell you what I hope I'll be doing. I hope I'll still be involved in football: preferably as a coach or a manager. That's all I can say. Football is the only life I've had, and the only life I can envisage.

Giggs is right to be a bit tetchy about the question. He's hardly started his career, after all. What we've seen of the Welshman so far should only be a taste of what is to come. Before we start to talk about Ryan Giggs the manager, with any luck there's a hell of a lot more to come from Ryan Giggs the player.

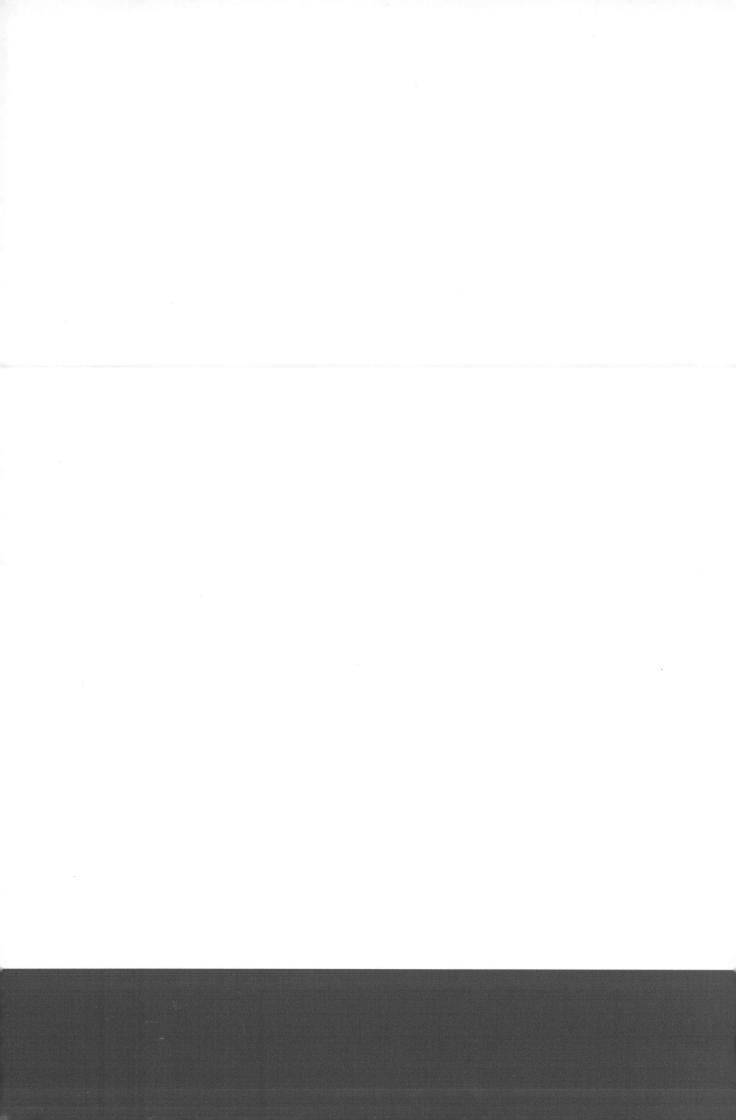

statistics

# 1990/1991

| Mar 2 | (H) | Everton | L | 0-2 | |
|---|---|---|---|---|---|
| May 4* | (A) | Man City | W | 1-0 | Giggs |

**Total league appearances: 2 (1) Goals: 1**

# 1991/1992

| Aug 17* | (H) | Notts Co | W | 2-0 | Hughes, Robson |
|---|---|---|---|---|---|
| Aug 24 | (A) | Everton | D | 0-0 | |
| Aug 28 | (H) | Oldham A | W | 1-0 | McClair |
| Aug 31* | (H) | Leeds U | D | 1-1 | Robson |
| Sep 7 | (H) | Norwich C | W | 3-0 | Irwin, McClair, Giggs |
| Sep 14 | (A) | South'ton | W | 1-0 | Hughes |
| Sep 21 | (H) | Luton T | W | 5-0 | Ince, Bruce, McClair 2, Hughes |
| Sep 28 | (A) | Tottenham | W | 2-1 | Hughes, Robson |
| Oct 6 | (H) | Liverpool | D | 0-0 | |
| Oct 19 | (H) | Arsenal | D | 1-1 | Bruce |
| Oct 26 | (A) | Sheff Wed | L | 2-3 | McClair 2 |
| Nov 2 | (H) | Sheffield U | W | 2-0 | Beesley (og), Kanchelskis |
| Nov 16 | (A) | Man City | D | 0-0 | |
| Nov 23 | (H) | West Ham | W | 2-1 | Giggs, Robson |
| Nov 30 | (A) | Crystal P | W | 3-1 | Webb, McClair, Kanchelskis |
| Dec 7 | (H) | Coventry C | W | 4-0 | Bruce, Webb, McClair, Hughes |
| Dec 15 | (A) | Chelsea | W | 3-1 | Irwin, McClair, Bruce |
| Dec 26* | (A) | Oldham A | W | 6-3 | Irwin 2, Kanchelskis, McClair 2, Giggs |
| Dec 29 | (A) | Leeds U | D | 1-1 | Webb |
| Jan 1* | (H) | QPR | L | 1-4 | McClair |
| Jan 11 | (H) | Everton | W | 1-0 | Kanchelskis |
| Jan 18 | (A) | Notts Co | D | 1-1 | Blackmore |
| Feb 1* | (A) | Arsenal | D | 1-1 | McClair |
| Feb 8 | (H) | Sheff Wed | D | 1-1 | McClair |
| Feb 22 | (H) | Crystal P | W | 2-0 | Hughes 2 |
| Feb 26 | (H) | Chelsea | D | 1-1 | Hughes |
| Feb 29 | (A) | Coventry C | D | 0-0 | |
| Mar 18* | (A) | Notts F | L | 0-1 | |
| Mar 21 | (H) | Wimbledon | D | 0-0 | |
| Mar 28 | (A) | QPR | D | 0-0 | |
| Mar 31 | (A) | Norwich C | W | 3-1 | Ince 2, McClair |
| Apr 7 | (H) | Man City | D | 1-1 | Giggs |
| Apr 16 | (H) | South'ton | W | 1-0 | Kanchelskis |
| Apr 18 | (A) | Luton T | D | 1-1 | Sharpe |
| Apr 20 | (H) | Notts F | L | 1-2 | McClair |
| Apr 22 | (A) | West Ham | L | 0-1 | |
| Apr 26 | (A) | Liverpool | L | 0-2 | |
| May 2 | (H) | Tottenham | W | 3-1 | McClair, Hughes 2 |

**Total league appearances: 38 (6) Goals: 4**

*EUROPEAN SUPER CUP*

| Nov 19 | (H) | Red Star Belgrade | W | 1-0 | McClair |
|---|---|---|---|---|---|

*RUMBELOWS LEAGUE CUP*
SECOND ROUND, FIRST LEG

| Sep 25 | (H) | Cambridge | W | 3-0 | Giggs, McClair, Bruce |
|---|---|---|---|---|---|

SECOND ROUND, SECOND LEG

| Oct 9 | (A) | Cambridge | D | 1-1 | McClair |
|---|---|---|---|---|---|

THIRD ROUND

| Oct 30 | (H) | Portsmouth | W | 3-1 | Robins 2, Robson |
|---|---|---|---|---|---|

FOURTH ROUND

| Dec 4 | (H) | Oldham A | W | 2-0 | McClair, Kanchelskis |
|---|---|---|---|---|---|

FIFTH ROUND

| Jan 8 | (A) | Leeds U | W | 3-1 | Blackmore, Kanchelskis, Giggs |
|---|---|---|---|---|---|

SEMI FINAL, FIRST LEG

| Mar 4 | (A) | Middlesbro | D | 0-0 | |
|---|---|---|---|---|---|

SEMI FINAL, SECOND LEG

| Mar 11 | (H) | Middlesbro | W | 2-1 | Sharpe, Giggs |
|---|---|---|---|---|---|

FINAL

| Apr 12 | | Notts Forest | W | 1-0 | McClair |
|---|---|---|---|---|---|

*FA CUP*
THIRD ROUND

| Jan 15 | (A) | Leeds U | W | 1-0 | Hughes |
|---|---|---|---|---|---|

FOURTH ROUND

| Jan 27 | (A) | South'ton | D | 0-0 | |
|---|---|---|---|---|---|

FOURTH ROUND REPLAY

| Feb 5 | (H) | South'ton | D | 2-2 | Kanchelskis, McClair |
|---|---|---|---|---|---|

# 1992/1993

| Aug 15 | (A) | Sheff U | L | 1-2 | Hughes |
|---|---|---|---|---|---|
| Aug 19 | (H) | Everton | L | 0-3 | |
| Aug 22 | (H) | Ipswich T | D | 1-1 | Irwin |
| Aug 24 | (A) | South'ton | W | 1-0 | Dublin |
| Aug 29 | (A) | Notts F | W | 2-0 | Hughes, Giggs |
| Sep 2 | (H) | Crystal P | W | 1-0 | Hughes |
| Sep 6 | (H) | Leeds U | W | 2-0 | Kanchelskis, Bruce |
| Sep 12 | (A) | Everton | W | 2-0 | McClair, Bruce |
| Sep 19 | (A) | Tottenham | D | 1-1 | Giggs |
| Sep 26 | (H) | QPR | D | 0-0 | |
| Oct 3 | (A) | Middlesbro | D | 1-1 | Bruce |
| Oct 18 | (H) | Liverpool | D | 2-2 | Hughes 2 |
| Oct 24 | (A) | Blackburn | D | 0-0 | |
| Oct 31 | (H) | Wimbledon | L | 0-1 | |
| Nov 7 | (A) | Aston Villa | L | 0-1 | |
| Nov 21 | (H) | Oldham A | W | 3-0 | McClair 2, Hughes |
| Nov 28 | (H) | Arsenal | W | 1-0 | Hughes |
| Dec 6 | (H) | Man City | W | 2-1 | Ince, Hughes |
| Dec 12 | (H) | Norwich C | W | 1-0 | Hughes |
| Dec 26 | (A) | Sheff Wed | D | 3-3 | McClair 2, Cantona |
| Dec 28 | (H) | Coventry C | W | 5-0 | Giggs, Hughes, Cantona, Sharpe, Irwin |
| Jan 9 | (H) | Tottenham | W | 4-1 | Cantona, Irwin, McClair, Parker |
| Jan 18 | (A) | QPR | W | 3-1 | Ince, Giggs, Kanchelskis |
| Jan 27 | (H) | Notts F | W | 2-0 | Ince, Hughes |
| Jan 30 | (A) | Ipswich T | L | 1-2 | McClair |
| Feb 6 | (H) | Sheff U | W | 2-1 | McClair, Cantona |
| Feb 8 | (A) | Leeds U | D | 0-0 | |
| Feb 20 | (H) | South'ton | W | 2-1 | Giggs 2 |
| Feb 27 | (H) | Middlesbro | W | 3-0 | Giggs, Irwin, Cantona |
| Mar 6 | (A) | Liverpool | W | 2-1 | Hughes, McClair |
| Mar 9 | (A) | Oldham A | L | 0-1 | |
| Mar 14 | (H) | Aston Villa | D | 1-1 | Hughes |
| Mar 20 | (A) | Man City | D | 1-1 | Cantona |
| Mar 24 | (H) | Arsenal | D | 0-0 | |
| Apr 5 | (A) | Norwich C | W | 3-1 | Giggs, Kanchelskis, Cantona |
| Apr 10 | (H) | Sheff Wed | W | 2-1 | Bruce 2 |
| Apr 12 | (A) | Coventry C | W | 1-0 | Irwin |
| Apr 17 | (H) | Chelsea | W | 3-0 | Hughes, Clarke (og), Cantona |
| Apr 21 | (A) | Crystal P | W | 2-0 | Hughes, Ince |
| May 3 | (H) | Blackburn | W | 3-1 | Giggs, Ince, Pallister |
| May 9* | (A) | Wimbledon | W | 2-1 | Ince, Robson |

**Total league appearances: 41 (1) Goals: 9**

*UEFA CUP*
FIRST ROUND, SECOND LEG

| Sep 29 | (A) | Torpedo M | D | 0-0 | |
|---|---|---|---|---|---|

*COCA-COLA CUP*
SECOND ROUND, SECOND LEG

| Oct 7 | (H) | Brighton | W | 1-0 | Hughes |
|---|---|---|---|---|---|

THIRD ROUND

| Oct 28 | (A) | Aston Villa | L | 0-1 | |
|---|---|---|---|---|---|

*FA CUP*
THIRD ROUND

| Jan 5 | (H) | Bury | W | 2-0 | |
|---|---|---|---|---|---|

JAN 23 (H) BRIGHTON W 1-0 GIGGS
FIFTH ROUND
FEB 14 (A) SHEFF U L 1-2 GIGGS

# 1993/1994

| AUG 15 | (A) | NORWICH C | W | 2-0 | ROBSON, GIGGS |
|---|---|---|---|---|---|
| AUG 18 | (H) | SHEFF U | W | 3-0 | KEANE 2, HUGHES |
| AUG 21 | (H) | NEWCASTLE | D | 1-1 | GIGGS |
| AUG 23 | (A) | ASTON VILLA | W | 2-1 | SHARPE 2 |
| AUG 28 | (A) | SOUTH'TON | W | 3-1 | IRWIN, SHARPE, CANTONA |
| SEP 1 | (H) | WEST HAM | W | 3-0 | BRUCE, SHARPE, CANTONA |
| SEP 11 | (A) | CHELSEA | L | 0-1 | |
| SEP 19 | (H) | ARSENAL | W | 1-0 | CANTONA |
| SEP 25* | (H) | SWINDON T | W | 4-2 | CANTONA, HUGHES 2, KANCHELSKIS |
| OCT 2 | (A) | SHEFF WED | W | 3-2 | HUGHES 2, GIGGS |
| OCT 16 | (H) | TOTTENHAM | W | 2-1 | SHARPE, KEANE |
| OCT 30 | (H) | QPR | W | 2-1 | CANTONA, HUGHES |
| NOV 7* | (A) | MAN CITY | W | 3-2 | CANTONA 2, KEANE |
| NOV 24* | (H) | IPSWICH T | D | 0-0 | |
| NOV 27 | (A) | COVENTRY C | W | 1-0 | CANTONA |
| DEC 4 | (H) | NORWICH C | D | 2-2 | McCLAIR, GIGGS |
| DEC 7 | (A) | SHEFF U | W | 3-0 | SHARPE, CANTONA, HUGHES |
| DEC 11 | (A) | NEWCASTLE | D | 1-1 | INCE |
| DEC 19* | (H) | ASTON VILLA | W | 3-1 | CANTONA 2, INCE |
| DEC 26 | (H) | BLACKBURN | D | 1-1 | INCE |
| DEC 29 | (A) | OLDHAM A | W | 5-2 | BRUCE, CANTONA, KANCHELSKIS, GIGGS 2 |
| JAN 1 | (H) | LEEDS U | D | 0-0 | |
| JAN 4 | (A) | LIVERPOOL | D | 3-3 | IRWIN, BRUCE, GIGGS |
| JAN 15 | (A) | TOTTENHAM | W | 1-0 | HUGHES |
| JAN 22 | (H) | EVERTON | W | 1-0 | GIGGS |
| FEB 5 | (A) | QPR | W | 3-2 | KANCHELSKIS, CANTONA, GIGGS |
| MAR 5 | (H) | CHELSEA | L | 0-1 | |
| MAR 14 | (H) | SHEFF WED | W | 5-0 | CANTONA 2, INCE, HUGHES, GIGGS |
| MAR 19 | (A) | SWINDON T | D | 2-2 | KEANE, INCE |
| MAR 22 | (A) | ARSENAL | D | 2-2 | SHARPE 2 |
| MAR 30* | (H) | LIVERPOOL | W | 1-0 | INCE |
| APR 2 | (A) | BLACKBURN | L | 0-2 | |
| APR 4 | (H) | OLDHAM A | W | 3-2 | INCE, GIGGS, DUBLIN |
| APR 16 | (A) | WIMBLEDON | L | 0-1 | |
| APR 23* | (H) | MAN CITY | W | 2-0 | CANTONA 2 |
| APR 27 | (A) | LEEDS U | W | 2-0 | KANCHELSKIS, GIGGS |
| MAY 1 | (A) | IPSWICH T | W | 2-1 | CANTONA, GIGGS |
| MAY 4 | (H) | SOUTH'TON | W | 2-0 | KANCHELSKIS, HUGHES |

**Total league appearances: 38 (6) Goals: 13**

*FA CUP*
FOURTH ROUND
JAN 30 (A) NORWICH W 2-0 KEANE, CANTONA
FIFTH ROUND
FEB 20 (A) WIMBLEDON W 3-0 CANTONA, INCE, IRWIN

SIXTH ROUND
MAR 12 (H) CHARLTON A W 3-1 HUGHES, KANCHELSKIS 2

SEMI FINAL
APR 10 OLDHAM A D 1-1 HUGHES
SEMI-FINAL REPLAY
APR 13 OLDHAM A W 4-1 IRWIN, KANCHELSKIS, ROBSON, GIGGS

FINAL
MAY 14 CHELSEA W 4-0 CANTONA 2, HUGHES, McCLAIR

*EUROPEAN CHAMPION CLUBS' CUP*
FIRST ROUND, FIRST LEG
SEP 15 (A) KISPEST W 3-2 KEANE, CANTONA

FIRST ROUND, SECOND LEG
SEP 29 (H) KISPEST W 2-1 BRUCE 2
SECOND ROUND, FIRST LEG
OCT 20 (H) GALATASARAY D 3-3 ROBSON, HAKAN (OG), CANTONA

SECOND ROUND, SECOND LEG
NOV 3 (A) GALATASARAY D 0-0

*COCA-COLA CUP*
SECOND ROUND, SECOND LEG
OCT 6 (H) STOKE CITY W 2-0 SHARPE, McCLAIR
THIRD ROUND
OCT 27 (H) LEICESTER C W 5-1 BRUCE 2, McCLAIR, SHARPE, HUGHES

FIFTH ROUND
JAN 12 (H) PORTSMOUTH D 2-2 GIGGS, CANTONA
FIFTH ROUND REPLAY
JAN 26 (A) PORTSMOUTH W 1-0 McCLAIR
SEMI FINAL, FIRST LEG
FEB 13 (H) SHEFF WED W 1-0 GIGGS
SEMI FINAL, SECOND LEG
MAR 2 (A) SHEFF WED W 4-2 McCLAIR, KANCHELSKIS, HUGHES 2

FINAL
MAR 27 ASTON VILLA L 1-3 HUGHES

# 1994/1995

| AUG 20 | (H) | QPR | W | 2-0 | HUGHES, McCLAIR |
|---|---|---|---|---|---|
| AUG 22 | (A) | NOTTS F | D | 1-1 | KANCHELSKIS |
| AUG 27 | (A) | TOTTENHAM | W | 1-0 | BRUCE |
| AUG 31 | (H) | WIMBLEDON | W | 3-0 | CANTONA, McCLAIR, GIGGS |
| SEP 11 | (A) | LEEDS U | L | 1-2 | CANTONA |
| SEP 17 | (H) | LIVERPOOL | W | 2-0 | KANCHELSKIS, McCLAIR |
| SEP 24 | (A) | IPSWICH T | L | 2-3 | CANTONA, SCHOLES |
| OCT 15 | (H) | WEST HAM | W | 1-0 | CANTONA |
| OCT 29 | (H) | NEWCASTLE | W | 2-0 | PALLISTER, GILLESPIE |
| NOV 6 | (A) | ASTON VILLA | W | 2-1 | INCE, KANCHELSKIS |
| NOV 10* | (H) | MAN CITY | W | 5-0 | CANTONA, KANCHELSKIS 3, HUGHES |
| DEC 17 | (H) | NOTTS F | L | 1-2 | CANTONA |
| DEC 26 | (A) | CHELSEA | W | 3-2 | HUGHES, CANTONA, McCLAIR |
| DEC 28 | (H) | LEICESTER C | D | 1-1 | KANCHELSKIS |
| DEC 31 | (A) | SOUTH'TON | D | 2-2 | BUTT, PALLISTER |
| JAN 3 | (H) | COVENTRY | W | 2-0 | SCHOLES, CANTONA |
| JAN 15 | (A) | NEWCASTLE | D | 1-1 | HUGHES |
| JAN 22 | (H) | BLACKBURN | W | 1-0 | CANTONA |
| JAN 25 | (A) | CRYSTAL P | D | 1-1 | MAY |
| FEB 4 | (H) | ASTON VILLA | W | 1-0 | COLE |
| FEB 11 | (A) | MAN CITY | W | 3-0 | INCE, KANCHELSKIS, COLE |
| FEB 22 | (A) | NORWICH C | W | 2-0 | INCE, KANCHELSKIS |
| FEB 25 | (A) | EVERTON | L | 0-1 | |
| MAR 4 | (H) | IPSWICH T | W | 9-0 | KEANE, COLE 5, HUGHES 2, INCE |
| MAR 7 | (A) | WIMBLEDON | W | 1-0 | BRUCE |
| MAR 15 | (H) | TOTTENHAM | D | 0-0 | |
| MAR 19 | (A) | LIVERPOOL | L | 0-2 | |
| MAR 22 | (H) | ARSENAL | W | 3-0 | HUGHES, SHARPE, KANCHELSKIS |
| APR 2 | (H) | LEEDS U | D | 0-0 | |

**Total league appearances: 29 (0) Goals: 1**

*FA CUP*
THIRD ROUND
JAN 9 (A) SHEFF U W 2-0 HUGHES, CANTONA
FOURTH ROUND
JAN 28 (H) WREXHAM W 5-2 IRWIN 2, GIGGS, McCLAIR, HUMES (OG)

FIFTH ROUND
FEB 19 (H) LEEDS U W 3-1 BRUCE, McCLAIR, HUGHES

SIXTH ROUND
MAR 12  (H)  QPR           W  2-0   SHARPE, IRWIN
SEMI FINAL
APR 9         CRYSTAL P     D  2-2   IRWIN, PALLISTER
SEMI FINAL REPLAY
APR 12        CRYSTAL P     W  2-0   BRUCE, PALLISTER
FINAL
MAY 20        EVERTON       L  0-1

*UEFA CHAMPIONS' LEAGUE*
SEP 14  (H)  IFK GOTH       W  4-2   GIGGS 2,
                                      KANCHELSKIS,
                                      SHARPE

SEP 28  (A)  GALATASARAY    D  0-0
NOV 2   (A)  BARCELONA      L  0-4

*UEFA CUP*
FIRST ROUND, FIRST LEG
SEP 12  (A)  ROTOR VOL      D  0-0
FIRST ROUND, SECOND LEG
SEP 26  (H)  ROTOR VOL      D  2-2   SCHOLES,
                                      SCHMEICHEL

*COCA-COLA CUP*
SECOND ROUND, FIRST LEG
SEP 20  (H)  YORK CITY      L  0-3
SECOND ROUND, SECOND LEG
OCT 3   (A)  YORK CITY      W  3-1   SCHOLES 2, COOKE

# 1995/1996

| | | | | | |
|---|---|---|---|---|---|
| AUG 26* | (H) | WIMBLEDON | W | 3-1 | KEANE 2, COLE |
| AUG 28* | (A) | BLACKBURN | W | 2-1 | SHARPE, BECKHAM |
| SEP 9* | (A) | EVERTON | W | 3-2 | SHARPE 2, GIGGS |
| SEP 16 | (H) | BOLTON | W | 3-0 | SCHOLES 2, GIGGS |
| SEP 23 | (A) | SHEFF WED | D | 0-0 | |
| OCT 1 | (H) | LIVERPOOL | D | 2-2 | BUTT, CANTONA |
| OCT 14 | (H) | MAN CITY | W | 1-0 | SCHOLES |
| OCT 21 | (A) | CHELSEA | W | 4-1 | SCHOLES 2, GIGGS, McCLAIR |
| OCT 28 | (H) | MIDDLESBRO | W | 2-0 | PALLISTER, COLE |
| NOV 4 | (A) | ARSENAL | L | 0-1 | |
| NOV 18 | (H) | SOUTH'TON | W | 4-1 | GIGGS 2, SCHOLES, COLE |
| NOV 22 | (A) | COVENTRY | W | 4-0 | IRWIN, McCLAIR 2, BECKHAM |
| NOV 27 | (A) | NOTTS F | D | 1-1 | CANTONA |
| DEC 17 | (A) | LIVERPOOL | L | 0-2 | |
| DEC 27 | (H) | NEWCASTLE | W | 2-0 | COLE, KEANE |
| DEC 30 | (H) | QPR | W | 2-1 | COLE, GIGGS |
| JAN 1 | (A) | TOTTENHAM | L | 1-4 | COLE |
| JAN 13 | (H) | ASTON VILLA | D | 0-0 | |
| JAN 22 | (A) | WEST HAM | W | 1-0 | CANTONA |
| FEB 3 | (A) | WIMBLEDON | W | 4-2 | COLE, PERRY (OG), CANTONA 2 |
| FEB 10 | (H) | BLACKBURN | W | 1-0 | SHARPE |
| FEB 21 | (H) | EVERTON | W | 2-0 | KEANE, GIGGS |
| FEB 25 | (A) | BOLTON | W | 6-0 | BECKHAM, BRUCE, COLE, SCHOLES 2, BUTT |
| MAR 4 | (A) | NEWCASTLE | W | 1-0 | CANTONA |
| MAR 16 | (A) | QPR | D | 1-1 | CANTONA |
| MAR 20 | (H) | ARSENAL | W | 1-0 | CANTONA |
| MAR 24 | (H) | TOTTENHAM | W | 1-0 | CANTONA |
| APR 6 | (A) | MAN CITY | W | 3-2 | CANTONA, COLES, GIGGS |
| APR 8 | (H) | COVENTRY | W | 1-0 | CANTONA |
| APR 13 | (A) | SOUTH'TON | L | 1-3 | GIGGS |
| APR 17 | (H) | LEEDS U | W | 1-0 | KEANE |
| APR 28 | (H) | NOTTS F | W | 5-0 | SCHOLES, BECKHAM 2, GIGGS, CANTONA |
| MAY 5 | (A) | MIDDLESBRO | W | 3-0 | MAY, COLE, GIGGS |

**Total league appearances: 33 (3)  Goals: 9**

*FA CUP*
THIRD ROUND
JAN 6   (H)  SUNDERLAND    D  2-2   BUTT, CANTONA
THIRD ROUND REPLAY
JAN 16  (A)  SUNDERLAND    W  2-1   SCHOLES, COLE
FOURTH ROUND
JAN 27  (A)  READING       W  3-0   GIGGS, PARKER, CANTONA
FIFTH ROUND
FEB 18  (H)  MAN CITY      W  2-1   CANTONA, SHARPE
SIXTH ROUND
MAR 11  (H)  SOUTH'TON     W  2-0   CANTONA, SHARPE
SEMI FINAL
MAR 31       CHELSEA       W  2-1   COLE, BECKHAM
FINAL
MAY 11       LIVERPOOL     W  1-0   CANTONA